DAN QUAYLE

AIRHEAD APPARENT

*A Fair, Unbiased Look
at Our Nation's Most
Dangerous Dimwit*

Paul Slansky
&
Steve Radlauer

Potatoe Press

DAN QUAYLE: AIRHEAD APPARENT

This book originated in an article commissioned by *Esquire*,
where much of it first appeared in different form. We
thank Terry McDonell, David Hirshey, Michael Hirschorn
and our other friends at the magazine.

Excerpt from *The Man Who Would Be President: Dan Quayle*
reprinted by permission of Simon & Schuster,
© 1992 by the Washington Post Co.

Embrace the Serpent, published by Crown Publishers, Inc., is
copyright © 1992 Marilyn T. Quayle and Nancy T. Northcott.

Cover Design by Andrea Sohn Design and Steve Radlauer
Cover Photo printed courtesy of AP/WIDE WORLD PHOTOS
ISBN 1-879682-30-3

Printed in the United States of America on recycled paper.

For information, please contact:

Potatoe Press
An imprint of Behind the News Press
1746 Shattuck Avenue, # 111
Berkeley, CA 94709

To David Beckwith,
who has the world's most impossible job:
making Dan Quayle look good.

CONTENTS

"Kakistocracy: Government by the worst men in the state."

—*Random House Dictionary of the English Language*

INTRODUCTION

Pablo Picasso dies and goes to Heaven, and God says, "To get into Heaven, you must prove to me you are who you say you are." So Picasso draws a picture and God lets him in. Next, Martin Luther King, Jr. dies, and God says, "Prove you are Dr. King." So he makes a long speech about civil rights and God lets him in. Then Dan Quayle dies, and God says, "Prove you're Dan Quayle." Quayle asks why. God says, "Because Pablo Picasso and Martin Luther King had to prove who they were." Quayle asks, "Who are they?" And God lets him in.

—**From a New York Times** *article on jokes children tell*

A t any point in the American zeitgeist, certain people are singled out for special comedic recognition. Their names become synonymous with the flaw or failure they embody. With no say in the matter, they are enlisted as national punchlines.

One's ascendance to this stature is often gradual. It took Richard Nixon a quarter century to fully realize his pariah potential, and the current eagerness to mock Nancy Reagan comes only after decades of her bad-vibe emissions. Occasionally, though, someone comes along whose utter inappropriateness is so obvious that he is instantly catapulted to the pinnacle of absurdity and sentenced to spend the rest of his life as a Cosmic Joke Butt. Such a man is our current vice president, J. Danforth Quayle.

Rarely has anyone made a less auspicious debut, lumbering onto the political scene as the embodiment of everything America claims not to stand for: a rich war-avoider spouting hawkish, tough-guy slogans; a lazy C-average frat boy whose blazing vapidity shone blindingly through his stunned blue eyes; a smug brat whose wit consisted entirely of schoolyard name-calling. That such a creature should be so close to the seat of power is the ultimate national joke, and everyone gets it. (Everyone, that is, but a hardy tribe of cheerleaders led by his alarming wife, his bellicose staff and his trusting hometown fans.)

"Hasn't Quayle been bashed enough?" you ask. Well, let us remind you of George Bush's fragile mortality—and the fact that a sitting vice president is ideally positioned to head the ticket the next time out. In other words, President Quayle, at the helm, sailing the Ship of State into the next millennium, is no more unthinkable today than President Reagan was...well, before he was President Reagan. So, to answer your question: No, he hasn't been bashed enough. Not nearly enough.

Quayle's watery baby-blues are already fixed on '96. Between now and November he'll be doing his darndest to convince us that he's a man of substance who's hung tough in the face of relentless media slashing and emerged a better, stronger, more compassionate human being. In short, that he's "grown in office."

Mercifully, few will buy into this impossible fantasy. As the campaign unfurls, the soul-baring lens of television will provide countless examples of Quayle *in flagrante delicto*—gesturing woodenly, grinning inanely, speaking foolishly. That is, just being himself. And it will be plain to all who care to notice that he is still *precisely the same clown we always thought he was.*

Of course, we could be wrong. And George Bush could be— to quote J. Danforth Quayle—"the most highly respected person not only in America but in the world."

Uh huh.

B.C. (BEFORE CONGRESS)

J ames Danforth Quayle was born in Indianapolis on February 4, 1947 to Corinne and James Quayle. James worked for Corinne's father, Eugene C. Pulliam, the potentate of Indiana's most powerful publishing empire, Central Newspapers. The Quayles lived in Huntington, Indiana (pop. 16,000) until 1955, when they moved to Scottsdale, Arizona. There young Dan learned to play golf. In 1963 they returned to Huntington, where Dan continued to play golf. He graduated from high school with mediocre grades, but no matter: DePauw University dropped its entrance standards for Dan as a courtesy to his parents and his influential grandfather, DePauw alumni one and all.

A FRAT HAWK

At DePauw, Dan played quite a bit of golf, monotonously spouted fierce pro-war, anti-Communist sentiments, and served on the fraternity-sorority social committee. He graduated in 1969 with a C average. Despite his hawkish posturing, our Dan had no intention of actually fighting in Vietnam. A Pulliam employee who happened to be the former state commander of the National Guard expeditiously procured for him an appointment to the Indiana Guard's headquarters detachment. It was a coveted assignment, characterized by ex-guardsmen as a "glory unit," a "dignitary unit." "These were top-notch people in this section," said a former member. "There were guys who were lawyers, accountants, district managers for corporations…" And one blond bimbo with connections.

Quayle, not previously known for his blowtorch stylings, was admitted to the unit as…*a welder*. He was given three months of welding training; then the invisible hand of influence gently deposited him in the 120th Public Information Unit—his apparent intended destination—the moment an opening appeared. He served out his term writing press releases, working on a Guard magazine (although not a single article appeared under his by-line), and, according to fellow guardsmen, keeping up a steady, obnoxious stream of pro-war cant. He spent the rest of his stint in the reserves, exiting in 1975.

CONFESSIONS OF A JOHN BIRCH DAD

James Quayle, a John Bircher and rabid Commiephobe (to whom meeting Birch founder Robert Welch was "like meeting the president of the United States"), was unfazed by his son's blatant hypocrisy. "At least he was in uniform," he told the *Washington Post.* "I saw him in uniform…I don't consider him a draft dodger or deserter." Who says family values are dead?

Dan's wife recalls the National Guard as his "transition point." To *what* she doesn't say. Certainly not to a quick study: after four years in the 120th, he took a test evaluating his skills in such areas as "fundamentals of writing" and "Army information." The average score was 75; he scored a 56.

PULLING STRINGS

In 1970, Quayle entered the Indiana University School of Law at Indianapolis. With his poor undergraduate record, the circumstances of his admission are highly suspect. Indeed, when he first sought admission "they wouldn't take him," James Quayle has said, loyally adding, "I don't think that's anything to be ashamed of." How did he get in? Some allege that, as usual, strings were pulled. Others say he was admitted under an affirmative action program for minority and disadvantaged students. As amusing as it is to speculate about the minority group he might have been deemed a member of—the intellectually challenged? the motivationally different? the low-handicapped? —we prefer James Quayle's version, which is that Dan "talked his way in" with his legendary golden-tongued glibness.

While at IU he met and married a fellow law student, the diligent Marilyn Tucker. He continued to play a good deal of golf. He was as unlikely a future world leader as Captain Kangaroo, or the Bee Gees, or (your name here).

DANNY, WE REALLY KNEW YA

On his smarts, his mediocrity, his suitability as a spouse

"He doesn't have the greatest smarts in the world."

—*James Quayle*

"I think that, obviously, I would not have married Dan Quayle had I not thought that he was an equal to me."

—*Marilyn Quayle*

"Dan Quayle was one of the few people able to get from the Deke house to the golf course without passing through a classroom...a crashingly mediocre student."

—*Robert Sedlack,*
DePauw English professor

"I was in college with the guy for three years and the only thing I remember is he was on the golf team and was quite a ladies' man....He was not a guy to take a position on anything except who his date was on Friday night and where to get drunk on Saturday night."

—*Clark Adams,*
DePauw classmate

"He was as vapid a student as I can ever recall....Nothing came out of his mouth that was worth remembering."

—*Michael Lawrence,*
DePauw political science professor

CONGRESSMAN QUAYLE

I n 1976, a small cabal of local Republican bigwigs who were friends of the Quayle family invited 29-year-old Dan to run for Congress in Indiana's Fourth District. They approached him simply because no qualified Republican was interested in losing to the popular Democratic incumbent, Ed Roush. Quayle's response: "I'll have to check with my dad." His dad's response: "Go ahead. You won't win."

Young Dan—endowed only with family connections, an unused law degree, a year's experience helping his dad run the 8,300-circulation *Huntington Herald-Press*, a golf-bred competitive streak, an aggressive grin, a ferocious wife, and the confidence of someone who lacks the good sense to appreciate his utter unsuitability to the task—jumped in.

WET HEAD

The timing was impeccable. Like voters across the nation, the people of the Fourth District were still reeling from Watergate and were highly susceptible to anti-incumbent campaign rhetoric. Quayle, looking like an overgrown child, with no track record in any field of endeavor, did not have to strain to prove he was a Washington outsider. Helped considerably by his wife's organizational skills and driving ambition, lavish contributions from New Right political action committees, his opponent's lazy campaigning, and his own prodigious handshaking abilities, Quayle surprised everyone and walked away with 55 percent of the vote.

As a member of the House, he quickly earned a reputation as a lightweight legislator and a heavy golfer. "His attendance record was lousy," said one of his aides. "They didn't know where he was a lot of the time. He'd be in the gym or he'd sneak off to play golf and they'd have to call all around to find him." Repeated sightings of him emerging from the House gym earned him the nickname "Wet Head." Nevertheless, two years later his constituents sent him back for a second term.

What kind of congressman was Quayle? Just the kind you'd expect of a kid who had never ventured beyond the narrow-minded, white-bread, right-wing atmosphere in which he was raised.

CONGRESSMAN QUAYLE WAS IN FAVOR OF:

Pollution:
- He voted to ease the auto emission standards of the Clean Air Act and reduce warranties on emission-control devices
- Voted to limit funding for energy conservation and solar energy R&D

Big Business:
- Voted to end federal controls on natural gas prices
- Voted against taxing oil companies on their windfall profits
- Voted against temporarily funding the Federal Trade Commission to avoid a shutdown

Human Rights Violators:
- Voted to let the Import-Export Bank continue dealing with countries deemed human rights violators by the Secretary of State

Private Schools:
- Voted to provide tax credits for people whose children attend private elementary and secondary schools

More Weapons:
- Voted to give the president discretion to authorize production of the neutron bomb
- Voted to maintain high funding levels for MX missile development
- Voted to allow production of chemical weapons

CONGRESSMAN QUAYLE WAS OPPOSED TO:

The Environment:
- He voted against creating national parks, wildlife refuges and nature preserves in Alaska
- Voted to reduce wilderness areas in Idaho

Women's Rights
- Voted to allow states to revoke ratification of the Equal Rights Amendment

Workers' Rights:
- Voted against indexing the minimum wage to the cost of living
- Voted to allow certain small businesses to ignore OSHA safety regulations

Consumer Rights:
- Voted against establishing an office to represent individuals before federal agencies and courts
- Voted against establishing a consumer co-op bank

Gay Rights:
- Voted to prohibit the Legal Services Corporation from assisting homosexuals who are denied rights because of their sexual orientation

Abortion Rights:
- Voted to prohibit federal funding of abortions

Domestic Programs:
- Voted against transferring billions of dollars from defense to domestic programs

SENATOR QUAYLE

Despite his campaign stance against incumbency, Quayle began thinking of ways to lengthen his stay and strengthen his power base in Congress early in his freshman season as a House member. By the middle of 1977, Dan and Marilyn were plotting the overthrow of three-term liberal Democratic senator Birch Bayh, who was up for reelection in 1980.

One inadequacy of which Quayle has never been accused is a lack of political cunning. Well before the 1980 campaign was in gear, he had convinced most of Indiana's influential Republicans to make him their second choice for 1980, the obvious first choice being incumbent Republican governor Doc Bowen. When Bowen declined to run—a move Quayle had anticipated—the fair-haired congressman with the poor attendance record took over as the Republican frontrunner.

"THE BOY'S RETARDED"

In his campaign, Quayle took aim at the same fat targets—high taxes, too much government, too much special-interest spending—that he had repeatedly bludgeoned in his congressional campaigns. He was also hawking the issue of term limitation—specifically, the term of Senator Bayh. Long-term members of Congress, he said to one group of young supporters, "become Washington people rather than people from Indiana. They move out there...they send their kids to school out there...they breathe the air out there, they drink the water out there, they become part of the Washington buddy system." According to Quayle, Bayh, after 18 years in Washington, was way out of touch with the needs of his constituents back home in Indiana. (The Quayles, incidentally, had bought a house in McLean, Virginia, in 1977. And, yes, they continued to breathe air, drink water, and send their children to school.)

Bayh considered Quayle a joke. Resisting his staff's suggestion that he prepare for a campaign debate, he once snapped, "C'mon boys, don't bother me. I'm debating Danny Quayle. The boy's retarded." But Danny's tactics, his glad-handing skills, and his fascinating ability to make eye contact with hundreds of people per minute paid off—regardless of his mental capacity or lack thereof. With the help of Ronald Reagan's capacious coattails, the kid dealt Bayh a 54 to 46 percent drubbing.

CONFLICT AVOIDANCE

While Quayle may not have had any actual goals when he entered the Senate, he had strong feelings about what he wanted to avoid. "I know one committee I don't want—Judiciary," he announced early on. "They are going to be dealing with all those issues like abortion, busing, voting rights, prayers. I'm not interested in those issues, and I want to stay as far away from them as I can." Another time he admitted, "I have very little interest [in civil rights]....My personal concerns are very minimal in that area."

His career in the Senate began with a bang: the report that the previous year he and two House colleagues had spent a Florida golf weekend rooming with lobbyist (and soon-to-be *Playboy* exhibitionist) Paula Parkinson. Dan proclaimed his innocence, Marilyn revealed that "anyone who knows Dan Quayle knows he would rather play golf than have sex any day," and the world soon turned its attention to less boring stories.

A BOISTEROUS SPEAKER

Senator Quayle's incumbency lasted eight years. (In 1986, the Indiana Democrats, scared off by his popularity and his enthusiasm for campaigning, ran a sacrificial no-name who lost by a wide margin.) According to the *Los Angeles Times*, Quayle was known in the Senate as a "boisterous" speaker whose face turned red and arms flapped wildly when he was excited about an issue. "Critics note," the *Times* continued, "that he frequently talks at length about issues whether he completely understands them or not....A congressional source remembers an incident in a closed committee meeting in which Quayle stood to propose an amendment but started to read from a paper on a different subject. He never realized it was the wrong paper until an aide approached and gave him the right one." And *The Making of a Senator: Dan Quayle*, by Richard F. Fenno, Jr., captures this Quayle apothegm on the difference between the two houses of Congress: "The

House is more informal. You can get a bunch of guys and go down to the gym and play basketball. You can't do that in the Senate."

HIS ACCOMPLISHMENT

In his eight years as a senator, Quayle accomplished one notable deed, and that early on: the Job Training Partnership Act of 1982. A modest, bipartisan program cosponsored by Quayle and diabolical archliberal Ted Kennedy, JTPA replaced the Comprehensive Employment and Training Act (CETA). Its purpose was, and is, to provide a budget and a mechanism for the training, in the private sector, of unemployed workers and unskilled youth. For this we tip our hats. Then, hats firmly back in place, we look at the rest of the Quayle senatorial oeuvre.

SENATOR QUAYLE WAS IN FAVOR OF:

Big Business:
- He voted to allow companies to close plants and declare mass layoffs without giving workers 60 days' advance notice

- Voted to allow companies to force job applicants to take lie-detector tests

Three-Martini Lunches:
- Voted not to increase the tax paid on business meals (the additional monies collected were to go to school lunch programs)

Human Rights Violators:
- Voted to halt debate on sanctions against South Africa, effectively blocking tougher sanctions

Private Schools:
- Again, voted to give parents tax breaks for sending their children to private schools

School Prayer:
- Voted to allow organized prayer sessions in public schools

Racial Discrimination:
- Favored tax exemptions for private schools practicing racial discrimination

The Pentagon:

- Voted not to reduce military programs by $49 billion. (*Arguing against proposed reforms of the Pentagon procurement system, Quayle once said, "In the past we have tried too much to prevent the making of mistakes."*)

More Weapons:

- Voted to spend more than $300 million on chemical weapons

- Voted to allow procurement or assembly of chemical weapons without Congressional approval

- Voted against a mutually verifiable weapons freeze and stockpile reduction in nuclear (which he pronounces as if it is spelled N-U-C-U-L-A-R) weapons

- Voted against reducing the MX missile program by $2.1 billion

- Voted to allow Star Wars (SDI) funding to rise

- Voted to allow interstate sales of handguns

- Voted to allow plastic firearms that cannot be detected by airport scanning machines

Dim Right-Wing Judges:

- Voted to confirm Daniel A. Manion as appeals court judge. (*Manion, who once cited among his 10 most significant cases the defense of a client accused of improperly repairing a VW Rabbit, was as notorious for his atrocious spelling, grammar and syntax as for his John Bircher father. [Sound familiar?] Said Quayle, who attended law school with Manion and therefore must know something we don't, Manion "epitomizes what we all like to see in jurisprudence." Defending Manion on Nightline, Quayle told Ted Koppel, "I'm not so sure that we want all those that graduated number one or number two in their class to be on...our federal judiciary. This is a diversified society."*)

Golf Pros:
- Introduced a bill to give golf pros a special tax break

SENATOR QUAYLE WAS OPPOSED TO:

The Environment:
- He voted against a toxic waste cleanup program

Women's Rights:
- Voted against a study of male-female pay disparities

Children:
- Voted not to fund the Women, Infants and Children program
- Voted not to fund school breakfasts and lunches
- Voted not to increase funding for childhood immunization programs
- Voted against funding for after-school child-care programs

Public Health and Safety:
- Voted to allow siting of nuclear waste dumps without regard for public health and safety

The United Nations:
- Voted to reduce U.S. contributions to the U.N.

Workers:
- Voted against a program to pay for workers' medical expenses associated with toxic dump cleanups
- Voted not to protect the seniority of employees of merged airlines
- Voted not to raise the minimum wage to $4.55

The Unemployed:
- Voted against extending unemployment benefits in states with high unemployment
- Voted not to provide $2.7 billion for health care benefits to the unemployed

People Who Aren't Rich:
- Voted against tax cuts for those earning under $50,000 a year

Veterans:
- Voted against providing disability payments to WWII veterans whose diseases resulted from exposure to nuclear weapons tests
- Voted to close mental health centers for Vietnam vets
- Opposed allowing veterans to participate in Job Training Partnership Act programs

Education:
- Voted to maintain Reagan cuts in elementary and secondary education
- Voted not to increase funding for education by $1.5 billion
- Voted against restoring Head Start funding
- Voted against funding a telecommunications network for teaching math, sciences and foreign languages
- Voted not to fund education for the disadvantaged

Civil Rights:
- He was one of only 14 senators to vote against the Civil Rights Restoration Act (the act that overturned the Supreme Court ruling that one branch of a private educational institution could discriminate while another branch received federal funds)

Cities:
- Voted to maintain Reagan cuts in urban development grants, mass transit, and community health centers

Abortion:
- Voted against federal funding for abortions
- Voted for a Constitutional amendment overturning *Roe v. Wade*

People with AIDS:

- Voted for a Jesse Helms amendment that allowed insurance companies to discriminate against people with AIDS

- Voted for another Helms amendment prohibiting AIDS research and education funding

Domestic Programs:

- Again voted not to transfer billions of dollars from defense to domestic programs

- Voted not to transfer $62 million from Star Wars to nutrition programs

"I AM THE FUTURE!"

The campaign for the vice presidency, 1988

July 21
George Bush predicts highly favorable reaction to upcoming announcement of running mate: "Everybody will say, 'What a fantastic choice.'"

August 13
Indiana Senator J. Danforth Quayle says being vice president would be "a good career move."

August 14
Quayle appears on *This Week with David Brinkley*, utters the name "George Bush" ten times in two minutes.

August 15
Quayle says only concern for his children kept him from entering presidential race.

August 16
Bush gets off riverboat in New Orleans, stuns nation with announcement of running mate, calling him "man of the future." Quayle leaps out of crowd and bounces up to podium like game-show contestant, grabbing at Bush and braying, "Let's go get 'em!" Rubs kiss from Barbara Bush off cheek.

★ ★ ★

Jeane Kirkpatrick calls Quayle "one of the brightest, most serious, and most well-informed young men in the Senate." Sen. John S. McCain (R-AZ) says, "A guy that good-looking just has to be attractive to women." Sen. Chic Hecht (R-NV) says, "He's hot. He's dynamite. Overnight, he'll become a national hero." Phyllis Schlafly says, "I was supporting Jack Kemp, but he sort of looks like Jack Kemp."

★ ★ ★

Bush campaign head James Baker III says, "The issue is not who might have been the very best qualified to be president. The issue is getting someone who is extremely well qualified to be president and might have some other attributes as well."

August 17

Quayle is asked why he joined National Guard instead of going to Vietnam, says: "Well, it's—growing up in Huntington, Indiana, the first thing you think about is education. You think about what any small-town person would think about—eventually growing up, raising a family. I was fortunate to be able to go on to law school, meet my wife. We have, I'm blessed with my three beautiful children. We're very happy, very content and looking forward to a very exciting campaign. I did not know in 1969 that I would be in this room today, I'll confess." Reporter asks again. Quayle replies, "My brother and I, two years younger, both went into the service at the same time, about the same time. He went into the Marine Corps and I went into the National Guard. I went into the National Guard and I served six years there from 1969 through 1975."

★ ★ ★

Quayle visits California delegation, declares, "The real question for 1988 is whether we're going to go forward to tomorrow or past to the—to the back!"

★ ★ ★

Quayle makes rounds of network anchor booths. Tells Peter Jennings, "I'm very proud of my service in the National Guard....There are really millions of Americans that have served in the National Guard." Tells Dan Rather, "I'm very proud of my service in the National Guard....There are really millions of people in America that are very proud to be part of the National Guard. I'm one of them." Tells Tom Brokaw, "I'm very proud of my service in the National Guard....There are millions of people in America that are very proud of their service in the National Guard." Says "phone calls were made" to facilitate his entry into Guard.

August 18

Washington Post reveals incorrect punctuation on Quayle's mail-box: "The Quayle's."

★ ★ ★

Quayle accepts vice-presidential nomination, says, "I don't presume to talk for everyone of my generation."

August 19

Quayle visits hometown of Huntington, Indiana. Explains why he asked parents to help get him into National Guard: "I do—I do—I do—I do what any normal person would do at that age: you call home. You call home to mother and father and say, 'I'd like to get in the National Guard.' " Refuses to say if he's offered to take his name off ticket because it's "not a yes or no question." Crowd boos media for having audacity to point out hypocrisy of loud support of Vietnam War and subsequent draft avoidance. Pia Zadora appears at rally, sings: "I'm just mad about George Bush, can't get my fill /Danny Quayle's looks give me a thrill."

August 20

Quayle campaigns in Ohio, warns that U.S. is "naked, absolutely nude to attack" by Soviets. Hecklers shout, "Quayle, Quayle called his Mom / Everybody else went to Nam."

August 21

Sen. Robert Dole (R-KS) says, "In my generation, you knew who was in the Guard and who was in uniform fighting for their country." Quayle attends church in Cleveland, encounters WWII vet who snarls, "You're a draft dodger!" Is pulled off campaign trail for crash course in what media calls "vice president school."

August 22

Quayle denies family influence helped him get into National Guard. Bush boldly defends running mate against unmade charges: "He did not go to Canada, he did not burn his draft card and he damn sure didn't burn the American flag!"

August 23

Quayle stages taking-out-the-trash photo op to deny Paula Parkinson's seven-year-old claim that he came on to her in Florida: "I hope there's some respect and dignity for things I did not do."

***

James Quayle says son's "main interests in school were broads and booze."

August 25

Quayle is asked about local farm issue, tells farmers, "Whatever you guys want, I'm for." Says his work on Senate Armed Services Committee involved getting cruise missiles "more accurate so that we can have precise precision."

August 26

Quayle refuses to release school records, blames inflated job description in resume on staff. Responds to question on farm policy by observing that "exports are very important."

August 27

Quayle explains his "intra-personal" relationship with Bush: "Although in public I refer to him as Mr. Vice President, in private I call him George. When he called, when I talked to him on the phone yesterday, I called him George rather than Mr. Vice President. But in public it's Mr. Vice President because that's who he is."

August 28

Quayle is asked who has run National Narcotics Border Interdiction System for past six years, is unaware that correct answer is "George Bush."

August 30

Jay Leno suggests title for movie on Quayle's Vietnam years: *Full Dinner Jacket.*

September 2

Quayle informs campaign rally, "This election is about who's going to be the next president of the United States!"

September 4

Quayle says he sees no difference between Gorbachev and past Soviet leaders: "Perestroika is nothing more than refined Stalinism."

September 8

Marilyn Quayle grants interview to *New York Times*, complains six times in one plane ride that she's "not getting paid" for serving as husband's chief adviser. Says husband "really is the studious sort" who "tries to read Plato's *Republic* every year," doesn't say if he ever succeeds. Claims FDR was a "lousy student" who "failed the bar exam seven times, for goodness' sake," though in fact he passed on first try.

★ ★ ★

Campaign manager Stuart Spencer lets Quayle wing it during speech so he'll make lots of gaffes and start sticking to the script: "I want him to step on his dick, and then we'll own him again."

★ ★ ★

Quayle attempts to cite pro-defense basketball philosophy, gets it backward: "Bobby Knight told me this: 'There is nothing that a good defense cannot beat a better offense.' In other words, a good offense wins." Cites Tom Clancy novel as justification for building strategic defense system, arguing, "Why wouldn't an enhanced deterrent, a more stable peace, a better prospect to denying the ones who enter conflict in the first place to have a reduction of offensive systems and an introduction to defensive capability. I believe that is the route this country will eventually go." Says Republicans "understand the importance of bondage between parent and child."

★ ★ ★

Lee Atwater says Quayle has "almost a rock star aura."

September 9

Quayle denies entry into law school was dependent on affirmative action program. Visits steel plant, tells T-shirted audience, "I can identify with steelworkers. I can identify with workers that have had a difficult time." Says he defended steel quotas in face-to-face encounter with Reagan by looking him "right across the eyes."

September 13
Quayle displays sophisticated wit: "Want to hear a sad story about the Dukakis campaign? The governor of Massachusetts, he lost his top naval adviser last week. His rubber ducky drowned in the bathtub."

September 15
Quayle calls Holocaust "an obscene period in our nation's history." Is told that Holocaust didn't take place in America, notes that he meant to say "in this century's history." Adds cryptically, "We all lived in this century. I didn't live in this century."

September 16
Quayle holds up Belgian endive in front of crowd, repeatedly crows "Endive!" as wife looks humiliated: "Endive! Endive! Remember that! Endive! Endive! Endive! Endive! Endive!"

September 17
Adviser describes Quayle as "the future standing right up there."

September 21
Quayle is urged by Barry Goldwater to "go back and tell George Bush to start talking about the issues." Declares, "We're going to have the best educated American people in the world." Refers to running mate as "George the Bush."

★ ★ ★

Marilyn Quayle says attraction to husband was based on his "intellectual curiosity."

September 23
Quayle explains vote against Iran trade embargo: "That particular vote was a vote where I did not think that the resolution on that

particular case would have been helpful." Audience giggles.

September 25
Marilyn Quayle is reported to be follower of far-right preacher and Armageddon buff, Col. Robert B. Thieme.

September 26
Bush campaigns with Quayle, says, "We cannot gamble with inexperience in that Oval Office."

★ ★ ★

Time runs photo of Quayle with fly resting between eyebrows.

October 4
University of Pennsylvania student shakes Quayle's hand, tells him, "You are such a weenie."

October 5
Quayle arrives at Omaha debate site for sound check, informs media that "The mike works. That's very important to make sure the mike works and ours is working well." Rehearses for debate, asks adviser Roger Ailes's permission to make gesture: "Hey Roger, does... on, on this, you know, if I'm gonna, if I, if I decide on my gesture over there...is that all right?...you don't mind?"

★ ★ ★

At debate, Quayle:

• Answers question about why people think he's a lightweight by reciting his qualifications for his prospective job

• Says next president "better understand about telemetry and acryption," though word is actually "encryption"

• Offers as proof of his "commitment" to the environment fact that "I take my children hiking and fishing, walking in the woods"

• Says his "commitment to the poor" once led him to visit people at food bank who were so "glad that I took time out of my schedule" that they didn't ask about his votes against programs that would have helped them

- Answers question about what he'd do if he became president by again reciting his qualifications

- Says it would be bad for economy if "we have another Jimmy Carter grain embargo, Jimmy, Jimmy Carter, Jimmy Carter grain embargo, Jimmy Carter grain embargo"

- Answers another question about first steps he'd take if he became president by yet again reciting his qualifications, among them that he knows Margaret Thatcher and Helmut Kohl and "they know me"

- Answers yet another question about actions he'd take upon assuming presidency by reciting his qualifications for fourth time, says he'll know Cabinet members "on a firsthand basis"

- Compares self to JFK once too often, is stunned by Lloyd Bentsen's rejoinder: "You're no Jack Kennedy"

- Answers question about "work of literature" that influenced him by citing three books he "read over the last spring vacation," among them a tome by noted literary stylist Richard Nixon

- Answers question about experience that shaped his political philosophy by citing bromide from grandmother (one of the richest women in America) that "You can do anything you want to if you just set your mind to it and go to work," then responds to audience laughter by claiming that they "sneer at that because it's common sense. They sneer at common sense advice. Midwestern advice. Midwestern advice from a grandmother to a grandson. Important advice. Something that we ought to talk about."

- Tells public, in conclusion, "You have been able to see Dan Quayle as I really am."

★ ★ ★

James Baker assesses Quayle's performance: "When you think about what might have happened, we have to be pretty happy."

October 6
Quayle explains repeated inability to tell debate audience what he'd do if he suddenly became president: "I had not had that question before."

October 7

Quayle sprays water at reporters "for all those stories you've been writing about me." Is asked about parents' ties to John Birch Society, calls question "ill-relevant." Is asked why, replies, "Because I said so!"

October 10

Quayle insists he really does know what to do if he becomes president: "Certainly I know what to do and when I am vice president—and I will be—there will be contingency plans under different situations. And I'll tell you what—I'm not going to go out and have a news conference about it, I'm going to put it in a safe and keep it there! Does that answer the question?"

★ ★ ★

Quayle declares independence from handlers after they tell media they have to "potty train" him: "I'm the handler...I am Doctor Spin." Reporters instantly assume that handlers told him to say it.

October 11

Quayle spots display of pumpkins in Ohio, shouts, "Pumpkin time!" Poses for photo holding one next to head.

October 13

Full-page ad appears in nation's newspapers demanding: "RELEASE DAN QUAYLE'S COLLEGE RECORDS NOW."

October 14

Quayle is asked which vice president he'll pattern himself after, almost forgets to say "George Bush."

October 18

Quayle announces, "I am the future!" Tells 11-year-old girl he'd want her to have baby if she was raped by her father: "You're a very strong woman....Though this would be a traumatic experience that you would never forget, I think that you would be very successful in life."

October 20

Quayle expounds on fall foliage: "We have gold and yellow and some red and, believe me, those are Republican colors. Bold colors, bright colors, future colors!" Explains that he calls rural America "real America" because, "It's rural America. It's where I came from. We always refer to ourselves as real America. Rural America, real America, real, real America."

★ ★ ★

Stuart Spencer complains about difficulties of running Quayle campaign: "First we had to shut that John Birch father of his up, and then the National Guard thing hit."

October 21

Comedian Albert Brooks campaigns for Dukakis, says, "Bush picked Quayle because he thought he would appeal to people in their 30s and 40s. Unfortunately, people with higher IQs don't seem to like him as much."

October 24

Quayle says he wouldn't want wife to have abortion if she was raped.

October 26

Quayle visits Miami high school with city's worst dropout rate, tells students, "We'll let the sunshine come in and shine on us, because today we're happy and tomorrow we'll be even happier." Bids audience "good night" at 10 a.m. Tells Cuban emigres, "We will invest in our people, quality education, job opportunity, family, neighborhood, and yes, a thing we call America."

October 27

Quayle addresses homeless problem: "I would guess that there's adequate low-income housing in the country." Suggests that government could help homeless by keeping interest rates down. Fails to explain how campaign promise of college education for anyone who wants one will be kept: "I haven't sat down and talked with George Bush on this, so I can't go in and tell you how we're going to do it."

October 28

Philadelphia Daily News refuses to endorse Bush because he "pretends, despite all the evidence, that J. Danforth Quayle is not a callow moron."

October 31

Quayle crashes through paper pumpkin at Michigan high school rally.

November 1

Quayle informs Ohio high school students that AIDS is "a very serious disease." Says Israel is "very important to the U.S."

November 2

Quayle, asked at Memphis senior citizens luncheon how his living arrangements would change if he's elected, says, "Well, it would sure be different to live in that White House." Questioner replies, "You're not the one who's running for president, now are you, Danny?" Is asked if woman raped by Willie Horton should have had his baby if she'd become pregnant. Says yes.

November 4

Convicted drug dealer Brett Kimberlin is placed in solitary confinement so he can't call prison press conference and claim he used to sell pot to Quayle.

November 5

Quayle campaigns at produce market in Baltimore suburb, tells crowd he and Marilyn were impressed by "the different types of little things that you could get for Christmas. And all the people that would help you, they were dressed up in things that said, 'I believe in Santa Claus.' And the only thing I could think is that I believe in George Bush."

November 6

Quayle attends Thanksgiving festival in Virginia, expresses gratitude for right of Americans "to elect the representatives to represent them in a free representative democracy."

November 7
Quayle goes unmentioned in GOP election-eve half-hour TV spot.

November 8
Quayle observes Election Day ritual of visiting dentist. Bush wins, 54% to 46%. Polls show Quayle cost ticket 2% of vote.

November 15
Sen. John Kerry (D-MA) jokes that Secret Service "is under orders that if Bush is shot, to shoot Quayle."

November 16
State dinner for Margaret Thatcher. Despite previous claim that he knows her, Quayle not invited.

November 17
Marilyn Quayle gives up quest to be named to husband's Senate seat. Says Indiana GOP pol, "I think the only person pushing her was her."

November 21
Nixon meets Quayle, says he's not an "intellectual midget."

November 30
Quayle says campaign taught him to talk less: "Verbosity leads to unclear, inarticulate things."

December 4
Private D.C. screening of *My Stepmother Is an Alien*. Quayle invited.

December 26
Bush defends annual quail-hunting trip: "These aren't 'animals,' these are wild quail....I don't think I could shoot a deer. Quail— that's something else again."

FIRST IMPRESSIONS

What we thought of him back in '88

"He seems like a figure fixed in time and place: a Friday afternoon in the late 1960s at the 'Deke' house at DePauw University. The beer keg has been tapped and Quayle and his fraternity brothers are leaning out of the second-story window leering at coeds. This is the man George Bush presents to us to fill the place once occupied by Theodore Roosevelt, Harry Truman and Hubert Humphrey."

—Ross K. Baker, Rutgers political science professor

"He's so light he could tapdance on a Charlotte Russe."

—Governor Mario Cuomo (D-New York)

"Bit of a quiz show host."

—John O'Sullivan, editor, National Review

"An ideological baloney sandwich."

—Kevin Phillips, GOP analyst

"He is not a ruminating creature. His nesting place is the mindless crowd, and his native woodnote the barbaric yawp....The back of Dan Quayle's head is beginning to bald and his pale eyes sit upon a balcony of crow's feet and there is the alarming suspicion that he will too soon be wrinkled and yet still be callow and too early grown old before he has really grown up."

—Murray Kempton, Newsday

"I'd like to see him spend just one night in the jungle. Don't even throw in the enemy. Just the elements."

—John LaPenta, Vietnam veteran

THE VALUED FAMILY

Dan waxes incoherent on his favorite subject

"We know what happens when families break up. We know what happens when you have, or when you don't have, a family. A family is very important, particularly to the children."

—*Quayle to* Tom Brokaw, *8/17/88*

"I've been very blessed with wonderful parents and a wonderful family, and I am proud of my family. Anybody turns to their family. I have a very good family. I'm very fortunate to have a very good family. I believe very strongly in the family. It's one of the things we have in our platform, is to talk about it."

—*Quayle to* Washington Post *reporter, 8/27/88*

"Don't forget the importance of the family. It begins with the family. We're not going to redefine the family. Everybody knows the definition of the family. A child. A mother. A father. There are other arrangements of the family, but that is a family and family values."

—*Quayle to Job Corps students, 9/28/88*

"I suppose three important things certainly come to my mind that we want to say thank you. The first would be our family. Your family, my family—which is composed of an immediate family of a wife and three children, a larger family with grandparents and aunts and uncles. We all have our family, whichever that may be....The very beginnings of civilization, the very beginnings of this country, goes back to the family. And time and time again, I'm often reminded, especially in this presidential campaign, of the importance of a family, and what a family means to this country. And so when you pay thanks I suppose the first thing that would come to mind would be to thank the Lord for the family."

—*Quayle ruminating about Thanksgiving, 11/6/88*

LOVE THAT MARILYN

No book about Dan Quayle would be complete without a personal look at the woman behind the man in the empty suit—Marilyn Quayle. Here are two close-up views:

MARILYN'S RELIGION

Two weeks before the '88 election, Larry King asked the soon-to-be Second Lady if she believed Jews were condemned to hell for not accepting Christ as their savior. Her response: "But all Jews have the opportunity to believe in the prophecies of the Bible."

"But if they don't?" King asked.

"That's a problem they have to deal with within their faith," she replied ominously.

Marilyn Tucker Quayle's attitude should come as no surprise. The Tucker clan was devoted to the ultraconservative preachings of Colonel Robert B. Thieme, a Houston minister who regularly attacks feminists, labor unions, welfare recipients, homosexuals, creeping socialism, rock 'n' roll, satanic propaganda and the United Nations, and who peddles wildly unorthodox Bible tapes with lurid titles like "Satanic Plot Number One" and "Slave Market of Sin." He is also fond of wearing his military uniform in the pulpit. Nancy Tucker Northcott, Marilyn's sister and writing partner, once admitted that their mother used to play his tapes "all day, every day." Another sister has said that Dan and Marilyn use the colonel's taped homilies to supplement the education of their children, Tucker, Benjamin and Corinne.

None of which should concern us in the slightest. According to Marilyn, she and her husband believe fervently, *fervently*, in the separation of church and state; should they happen one day to find themselves the occupants of 1600 Pennsylvania Avenue, they wouldn't dream of imposing their beliefs on even the most blasphemous freethinking heathen among us.

MARILYN'S TEMPER TANTRUM

A recent incident reported in The Man Who Would Be President: Dan Quayle *by Bob Woodward and David S. Broder:*

"On the wall was a large photograph of [Quayle] finishing a golf swing. His shirt had gathered and filled at his stomach, suggesting a paunch. 'You can't have that up there,' Marilyn Quayle said she remembers saying. 'It's terrible...Take it down...Look at that stomach!'...She picked up a pen and began scribbling out her husband's image with deep, heavy strokes, first the midsection and then the rest of him. 'I made it so you couldn't see who it was,' she recalled.

"At first, said one of the women who witnessed the incident, 'We took it pretty much as a joke...but it got very intense....It did flash through my mind: She's taking a lot out on that picture.'...An eyewitness said that Marilyn Quayle then placed the picture on the floor and, 'She kicked it.'...Her final words, all agreed, were, 'I don't want to ever see this again.'...In an interview, one of the eyewitnesses said, 'To do it in front of all of us. I've seen some pretty goofy things, but nothing like this....Human behavior is a strange thing.'

"In a final half-hour interview in which she spoke about the picture incident and other matters, she described it as a 'lark,' and a joke that had been misinterpreted.

"But during the interview, she became alternately distraught and indignant over the prospect of the incident becoming public. At several points, her voice quavered and she became tearful.

" 'I don't lose my temper very often,' she said. 'I am not a violent person.' "

GROAN IN OFFICE

Dan Quayle's vice presidency, 1989

January 17
CNN/*Time* poll shows 52% of Americans think Vice President-elect Quayle unqualified to assume presidency.

January 20
Justice O'Connor administers oath of office to Quayle, accidentally leaves out line. Departing Reagan helicopter blows Marilyn's hat, which resembles dog-food dish, off head.

January 31
Quayle tells reporters U.S. "condones violence in El Salvador."

February 1
QUAYLE SCARE!—Bush gets laryngitis.

February 3
Quayle visits El Salvador, says U.S. expects local officials "to work toward the elimination of human rights."

March 2
With GOP National Committee having censured views of Louisiana state legislator David Duke, Quayle commends party for its "censorship" of former Klansman.

March 10
Quayle accuses Democrats who defeated nomination of John Tower as defense secretary of loosing "a new wave of McCarthyism in this country."

March 13
Quayle gloats that he now has upper hand over political enemies: "I'm the vice president. They know it, and they know that I know it."

March 16

Quayle says *The Satanic Verses* is "obviously not only offensive but, I think, most of us would say, in bad taste," though he hasn't read it.

March 31

Bush establishes President's Council on Competitiveness, an agency dedicated to furtive undoing of environmental and safety regulations that big business finds onerous. Names Quayle chairman.

April 1

Quayle ridiculed at Gridiron Dinner. Wife glares at joke tellers.

April 5

USA Today reports Quayle's bold praise of a pastime popular with his boss: "Great American sport. Horseshoes is a very great game. I love it."

April 17

Quayle meets with editors of *Charlotte Observer*. Paper writes, "Like most Americans, we could have drawn up a long list of names of people qualified to be vice president, and J. Danforth Quayle wouldn't have been on it. Well, we talked with him Monday. His name still wouldn't be on it."

April 24

Quayle visits Chicago school, tells students: "We will move forward, we will move upward, and, yes, we will move onward."

★ ★ ★

Rep. Claudine Schneider (R-RI) jokes that Quayle told her, "I was recently on a tour of Latin America, and the only regret I have was that I didn't study Latin harder in school so I could converse with those people." News media takes her seriously, reports quote as real.

April 25

Quayle visits Hawaii: "Hawaii has always been a very pivotal role in the Pacific. It is in the Pacific. It is a part of the United States that is an island that is right here." Travels to American Samoa, tells natives, "You all look like happy campers to me. Happy campers you are, happy campers you have been, and, as far as I am concerned, happy campers you will always be." Arrives in Pago Pago, calls it "Pogo Pogo."

April 30
Quayle insists on getting in one more tennis game and snorkel dive at Jakarta luxury resort. Arrives two hours late for meeting with Indonesian vice president.

May 1
Marilyn Quayle announces her pet project: disasters.

May 2
Quayle plays too long at Singapore golf course, arrives late for meeting with prime minister. Aide tells reporter, "You can tell from the way he plays golf that he's a natural leader."

May 4
Quayle grants interview to *U.S. News & World Report*, laments, "Every once in a while, you let a word or phrase out and you want to catch it and bring it back. You can't do that. It's gone, gone forever."

May 5
Quayle inspects Exxon *Valdez* oil spill, exhorts cleanup workers to "have a great day."

May 8
Quayle receives honorary degree from Fisk University, says the historically black Nashville institution has made "the greatest comeback since Bill Cosby returned to network television."

May 9
Quayle addresses United Negro College Fund, attempts to quote slogan, "A mind is a terrible thing to waste." Says, "'What a waste

it is to lose one's mind,' or, 'Not to have a mind is being very wasteful.' How true that is."

May 19
Quayle declares, "This administration stands for the future. It also stands for what's good about this country."

May 22
Quayle declares, "I believe we are on an irreversible trend toward more freedom and democracy—but that could change."

May 24
Quayle addresses West Point graduating class. Spokesman David Beckwith says cadets "made an animal-type grunting sound when the National Guard was mentioned. There were some good-natured grunts. Let me admit theoretically that some people hissed."

June 13
Quayle poses in El Salvador with grenade launcher aimed, unbeknownst to him, at own elbow.

July 15
Quayle addresses Young Republicans National Convention, notes upcoming 20th anniversary of moon walk. Refers to astronaut Buzz Aldrin as "Buzz Lukens," an Ohio congressman recently given 30 days in jail for having sex with 16-year-old girl.

July 16
Witcover/Germond campaign book, *Whose Broad Stripes and Bright Stars?*, reports derisive comments by several of Quayle's aides about the candidate's "immaturity and lack of attention."

July 20
Quayle addresses 20th anniversary celebration of moon landing: "Welcome to President Bush, Mrs. Bush and my fellow astronauts."

August 11
Quayle explains why he favors sending humans to Mars: "Mars is

essentially in the same orbit. Mars is somewhat the same distance from the sun, which is very important. We have seen pictures where there are canals, we believe, and water. If there is water, that means there is oxygen. If oxygen, that means we can breathe." Spokesman Beckwith rushes forth, assures public Quayle "obviously knows there's no water flowing in the canals now."

August 15

Quayle defends Bush's civil rights record at opening of Southern Christian Leadership Conference convention, rattles off list of black heroes and civil rights victories. Audience members roll their eyes.

August 17

Quayle tells Sam Donaldson, "I stand by all the misstatements that I've made."

October 2

Quayle declares, "Japan is an important ally of ours. Japan and the United States of the Western industrialized capacity, 60 percent of the GNP, two countries. That's a statement in and of itself."

October 16

Quayle attends Seattle event promoting Ted Turner's Goodwill Games, says, "There is a future in the Games in the future."

October 18

Quayle—decked out in blue blazer with gold lettering identifying him as "Dan Quayle, Vice President of the U.S."—inspects quake-ravaged San Francisco. Says he "couldn't help but be impressed by the magnitude of the earthquake," calls it "heart-rendering sight." Adds, "The loss of life will be irreplaceable." Local resident heckles, "Don't worry, Dan, nothing happened to the golf course."

November 4

White House aide claims Quayle was central strategist for Bush's key first-year efforts to cut capital gains tax, obtain full budget request for SDI, and confirm John Tower as defense secretary. Aide fails to note Bush was unsuccessful in all three.

December 1

With Bush en route to Malta summit during Philippines crisis, White House aide alerts media that Quayle, staying very, very late in situation room, "ran effective meetings" and "asked the right questions."

December 6

Quayle tells Larry King, "One word sums up probably the responsibility of any vice president, and that one word is 'to be prepared.'" Marvels that "Dubcek, who brought the tanks in in Czechoslovakia in 1968 is now being proclaimed a hero," though in fact Dubcek was key figure in resisting invasion.

December 21

Media reports that Quayles sent out 30,000 Christmas cards with misspelled message: "May our nation continue to be the beakon of hope to the world." Quayle gives Bush toilet-paper holder that plays "Hail to the Chief" when paper is unrolled.

December 26

Mirabella magazine calls Marilyn's hairdo "the worst of the millennium."

December 30

Quayle tells Associated Press he spends "a great deal of time" with Bush, is "not, as they say, a potted plant in these meetings." Says he could take over "if that tragic event should occur" because he knows "what the president does on a day-to-day basis, how he goes about the job. I'm there. I'm present....Believe me, I know what to do."

GROAN IN OFFICE II

Dan Quayle's vice presidency, 1990

January 10
Quayle Quarterly, magazine devoted to mockery of veep, begins publication. Says spokesman Beckwith, "I had hoped it would be a scholarly publication studying the vice president and the vice presidency. But this is on the level of a high school humor magazine."

February 15
With Bush risking life attending drug summit in Colombia, Quayle visits drug-ravaged D.C. neighborhood. Resident asks, "Bush ain't dead, is he?"

March 11
Quayle stops at Chilean coastal village for souvenirs, buys South American Indian doll with enormous erection. Tells Marilyn, "This is something teenage boys might find of interest."

March 13
Quayle plants tree at residence of American ambassador to Paraguay, notes it's been 32 years since anyone has done this: "I was 11 then. I remember reading it in the *Weekly Reader*, how Vice President Nixon planted a tree here, and I always wanted to do that. It's true. I was 11 years old. I read it." Visits frigate in Buenos Aires. Ship's captain tells him, "We haven't had time to get you a respectful gift," presents him with empty box.

March 14
Gallup poll shows 54% of Americans think Quayle unqualified to assume presidency.

March 19
Quayle boasts that he knows Latin American leaders "by their first names."

March 23

✳ Quayle declares, "If we do not succeed, then we run the risk of failure."

April 5

Michael Jackson drops by Quayle's office. Aide reports they "hit it off famously."

April 9

Hit the Trail for Quayle Club launches letter-writing campaign to late-night talk show hosts telling them to stop making fun of him. Says founder Dorothy Vallosio, "The public is being programmed to think our vice president is a laughingstock."

May 1

Quayle warns of danger of asteroids crashing into Earth: "It would certainly benefit all nations to know when such a natural event might occur....Those same asteroids which promise material riches can be a threat as well."

May 9

Several members of American Legion of Paris boycott American Embassy ceremony to protest presence of perceived draft-dodger Quayle.

May 20

Quayle discusses his prospects for remaining on ticket: "1992 is a long time away....There is a public out there still willing to want to know who I am."

June 6

Man shouting "I have documents!" throws sheaf of papers at Quayle, hits him in head.

July 18

Quayle tells North Carolina audience, "Even though federal health officials are promoting less tobacco use, the tobacco industry should continue to expand in foreign markets." Says U.S. is "not going to deny a country an export from our country" just because it's deadly.

September 5
Quayle delivers morale-boosting speech to NASA employees, declares, "For NASA, space is still a high priority."

September 18
Quayle delivers speech on education, observes, "Quite frankly, teachers are the only profession that teach our children."

September 22
Quayle says of volatile Middle East situation, "We are ready for any unforeseen event that may or may not occur."

September 26
Quayle announces support for efforts "to limit the terms of members of Congress, especially members of the House and members of the Senate."

October 2
Quayle goes on *Nightline*, explains that there is no parallel between Vietnam and the Middle East because "Vietnam is a jungle. You had jungle warfare. Kuwait, Iraq, Saudi Arabia, you have sand." Says there's no need to worry about a protracted war because "from an historical basis, Middle East conflicts do not last a long time."

October 9
Quayle visits elementary school, assures four-year-old girl that he has access to Bush: "I work with the president almost on a daily basis. I was with him until 6:30 last night. I'll be with him Thursday morning. We talk every day."

October 12
Quayle comments on David Duke's prospects in Louisiana Senate race: "Unfortunately, the people of Louisiana are not racists."

October 24

Sidney Blumenthal's *Pledging Allegiance* reveals taped rehearsal Quayle had with media consultant in 1980: "I'm Dan Quayle. I'm Dan Quayle. I'm Dan Quayle. I am Dan Quayle. The real Dan Quayle. The real Dan Quayle stand up. I'm Dan Quayle. I'm Dan Quayle."

November 5

Quayle plays self on episode of *Major Dad*.

November 8

Quayle says that he and Defense Secretary Dick Cheney "have something in common. That is that we both overmarried."

December 28

Quayle golfs at all-white country club in Pebble Beach, claims not to have known of discrimination though club dropped out of PGA Tour rather than accept minority members. Says Chief of Staff Bill Kristol, "It proves he's not spending time reading the golf pages."

December 30

Quayle says he's sorry he golfed at club that excludes blacks, but will still play at D.C. course that excludes women: "I've played there before and I'll play there again....There are a lot of other very well-respected people that have played at Burning Tree."

December 31

Quayle visits combat-ready U.S. troops in Saudi Arabia, repeats over and over, "This will not be another Vietnam." Observes comedian Harry Shearer, "He was never near Vietnam, so if this was another one, how would *he* know?"

GROAN IN OFFICE III

Dan Quayle's vice presidency, 1991

January 3
Columnist Richard Cohen defines "Quayle bashing" as "the term used by the vice president's defenders whenever someone points out that the man is a fool."

February 4
Friends of Dan Quayle throws its hero surprise 44th birthday party. Says member Emily White, "I think he accurately expresses the views of most Americans."

March 3
Unnamed Bush aide says of Quayle's tenure, "It didn't turn out quite as we had planned and hoped."

April 11
Quayle hails America's Gulf triumph as "a stirring victory for the forces of aggression."

May 4
QUAYLE SCARE!—Bush suffers irregular heartbeat, checks into Bethesda Naval Hospital.

May 6
QUAYLE SCARE!—Bush prepares for temporary transfer of powers to Quayle. Anesthesia proves unnecessary, thyroid condition diagnosed.

May 9
CBS News/*New York Times* poll shows 62% of Americans "worried about" idea of Quayle as president.

May 11

Premier Dan Quayle Memorabilia Exhibit begins 10-day run in room at Huntington, Indiana, public library. Among items on display: coffee cup he once drank from, chair he once stood on, official airsickness bag from '88 GOP convention, swatch of carpeting former housekeeper saved from one of his floors, poem he wrote at 13 ("My Dad is very very nice / But he is not made of sugar and spice / Sometimes he acts as if he has been disturbed / But at other times he is as cheerful as a bird.")

May 13

Newsweek cover asks of Quayle, "Is He a Lightweight— Or Smarter Than You Think?" Prompts reader Susan Westenbarger to write, "Quayle could be much smarter than I think and still be a lightweight."

May 15

Marilyn Quayle denies that husband needs to change his image: "I don't think Dan needs to reconstruct anything. He needs to be covered fairly...but I certainly no longer expect that."

June 15

Quayle hosts five-kilometer race to benefit cancer research, tells fellow runners, "I appreciate your all participating in this 5,000-kilometer run."

July 12

Bush lashes out at senators backing off from initial support of Robert Gates for CIA chief, says without irony, "You hear a rumor and then you run for cover. You get under the bush like a quail and hope that you don't get flushed out for a while."

July 17

The Nation, reporting on Quayle's role as head of President's Council on Competitiveness, says his domestic policy experience "appears to be largely limited to undercutting safeguards that protect public health."

August 13
Lawyer Quayle addresses American Bar Association, complains there are too many lawyers.

August 27
Producers of ABC late-night talk show *Into the Night* cancel two guests specializing in Quayle mockery. Source says "broadcasting-standards guys have told us to lay off Quayle."

September 24
Quayle is praised for recent attacks on legal profession, declares, "The lawyers today, the media tomorrow."

October 8
Quayle woos pro-choice GOP voters, says, "We do, in former chairman Lee Atwater's words, offer the party as a big tent, and therefore that message has to be clear. How we do that within the platform, the preamble to the platform or whatnot, that remains to be seen. But that message will have to be articulated with great clarity." Later explains that "the big tent is a pro-life big tent." London-based Plain English Campaign gives Quayle its annual Doublespeak Award for quote.

October 11
Marilyn Quayle reveals she's been victim of sexual harassment and that in all instances, "I point-blank nipped it in the bud."

November 3
WWII hero Richard McCool drops out of Congressional Medal of Honor Society because organization is presenting Patriot Award to Quayle.

November 8
Quayle comments on Magic Johnson AIDS story: "If there is something that I can personally do to encourage young people, I would say not 'safe sex,' I would talk about abstinence. That's a sure cure and we ought to be talking about it. It's the proper response. I think there is a lot of virtue in abstinence."

November 11

Doonesbury begins two-week storyline revealing previously secret 1982 investigation into charges—ultimately unsubstantiated—that Quayle used cocaine and Quaaludes.

November 15

Quayle tells Christian group about need for abstinence to avoid AIDS: "My friends, no matter how rough the road may be, we can and we will never, never surrender to what is right."

November 17

Quayle, on *This Week with David Brinkley*, refers to possible candidate Cuomo three times as "Maaarrrio," slyly emphasizing weird foreignness of potential Bush opponent.

November 19

Cuomo calls Quayle "Danny the cabin boy for the captain of the Titanic."

December 6

Quayle says of John Sununu's departure from White House, "This isn't a man who is leaving with his head between his legs."

December 27

Bush hunting party kills 29 quail.

GROAN IN OFFICE IV

Dan Quayle's vice presidency, 1992

January 5

Massive seven-part Woodward/Broder series attempting to take Quayle seriously starts in *Washington Post*.

January 8

QUAYLE SCARE!—Bush, in Tokyo, vomits in lap of Japanese prime minister, collapses to floor. Quayle, asked in New Hampshire about his fitness to take over presidency, declares, "I'm ready." Tells crowd, "You didn't make a mistake by electing Ronald Reagan in 1980 and 1984, and you didn't make a mistake by electing George Bush in 1988, and you're not gonna make a mistake by electing anyone else besides George Bush in 1992."

January 9

Quayle defends space program: "Think of all the things we rely upon in space today. Communications from Japan. Detection of potential ballistic missile attacks. Ballistic missiles are still there. Other nations do have ballistic missiles. How do you think we were able to detect some of the Scud missiles and things like that? Space. Reconnaissance. Weather. Communications. You name it. We (pause) use (pause) space (pause) a lot (pause) today. And we're going to continue."

January 10

Woodward/Broder series in *Post* finally comes up with memorable scene: the Marilyn Quayle tantrum in which she demanded that an unflattering photo of her husband be removed from his office wall, then scribbled over his image, kicked it to remove it from frame, and tore it to bits.

January 12

Woodward/Broder series concludes with report that, when asked if he had any black friends or staff members he regularly consults with, Quayle replied, "Well, Carolyn Washington runs the house, and we see her every day."

January 16
Quayle says Woodward/Broder series rescued him from buffoondom: "No serious journalist can ever again write the Jay Leno caricature." Says Bush will "lead us out of the recovery."

January 17
Quayle spots "Now Hiring" sign in window of California Burger King, cites it as proof that economy is "beginning to turn around." Fact that available jobs are part-time at minimum wage ($4.25 an hour) doesn't deter his optimism: "You have a part-time job, you have a job. That's better than no job at all."

January 19
Columnist Murray Kempton notes Marilyn Quayle's comment to Woodward/Broder that husband "can't read a speech," writes, "Vice presidents have no visible employment except reading aloud; and now, it seems, we would demand too much if we asked this one to perform that minimal chore acceptably."

January 21
Columnist Russell Baker responds to Woodward/Broder series, asks, "Why do serious people keep saying Dan Quayle is 'not as bad as he's made out to be?' The question isn't what degree of badness Quayle measures out at....Why doesn't anybody ever say, 'Dan Quayle would make a great president?' "

January 24
NBC News/*Wall Street Journal* poll shows 62% of Americans "uncomfortable with" idea of Quayle as president.

February 1
Quayle stops into New Hampshire Dunkin' Donuts for frozen yogurt, asks how business is. Owner says it would be better without Quayle and Secret Service agents blocking counter.

February 23
On *Meet the Press,* Quayle denies that Willie Horton ad was example of negative advertising, denies that he joined National Guard "to avoid going to Vietnam," and denies that Bush broke his read-my-lips-no-new-taxes campaign promise by signing tax hike in 1990.

March 24
Marilyn Quayle and sister begin 11-city book tour for their first "thriller," *Embrace the Serpent,* in which hero—a black Republican senator—triumphs over stupid Democratic president, craven libidinous journalists, godless communists. Book—which *Publishers Weekly* cites for its "Democrat-bashing, tin-ear dialogue...soapbox-style narration...painful prose and political point-making"—contains no sex scenes despite kinky title.

March 26
QUAYLE SCARE!—Four growths removed from Bush's face. Doctor says president needs vacation.

April 13
Caller identifying himself as "Dave" phones San Antonio radio talk show to attack Brett Kimberlin, who's on the air from prison repeating claims to have sold pot and Quaaludes to Quayle in 1970s.

April 15
Quayle spokesman Beckwith acknowledges that he was "Dave," says he didn't give his last name or occupation because no one asked.

April 20
People reports that Quayle's office turned down National Kidney Foundation request for contribution of doodle for charity auction, sent autographed photo with note explaining that "due to his hectic schedule the vice president cannot afford you a doodle."

★ ★ ★

Quayle blows whistle at White House Easter Egg Roll.

April 29

Village Voice writer Mim Udovitch reviews *Embrace the Serpent*, says, "Readers hungry for a book by a woman who has only made it into print by virtue of her marriage to a near-universally despised man would be far better advised to check out Ivana Trump's *For Love Alone*."

April 30

Quayle visits Bellevue Hospital in New York, asks administrators if AIDS patients are "taking DDT."

May 19

Quayle, in San Francisco, cites *Murphy Brown*'s "mocking the importance of fathers" as example of bad Hollywood values that resulted in "lawless social anarchy" of L.A. riots. *Murphy Brown* creator Diane English responds, "If the vice president thinks it's disgraceful for an unmarried woman to bear a child, and if he believes that a woman cannot adequately raise a child without a father, then he'd better make sure abortion remains safe and legal."

★ ★ ★

Protester alleges that Quayle spokesman Beckwith hit him with "a wimpy punch" during pre-speech altercation. Beckwith denies charge.

May 20

Quayle takes time out from fund-raising at country clubs to tour South Central L.A., attacks Hollywood types for living in "the world of comfort. They ought to come with me out to where the real America is." Defends attack on *Murphy Brown*: "Illegitimacy is something that we should talk about in terms of not having." Says teenage onlooker: "He's not, like, smart. I'm not trying to bag on him or anything, but he has the same mentality I have—and I'm in the eighth grade."

May 27

Washington Post reports that Quayles rent their McLean, Virginia, home to unmarried couple. Spokesman says Quayles "were not involved at all in the rental negotiations."

May 29

Gallup poll for *Entertainment Weekly* shows public, by 43%-32% margin, thinks Murphy Brown "would make a better parent" than Quayle, and, by 40%-38% margin, "would make a better president."

June 7

ABC News/*Washington Post* poll shows 54% of Americans have unfavorable opinion of Quayle, 63% think him unqualified to assume presidency—his worst ratings yet in this poll.

June 8

Wall Street Journal reports Quayle is reading *The Autobiography of Malcolm X* in search of clues to the causes of and cures for racial conflict.

June 9

Quayle attacks "cultural elite," declares, "I wear their scorn as a badge of honor."

June 10

Quayle visits Long Island community center, plays basketball in tassled loafers. Brags he knows "exactly who the cultural elite, the media elite and the Hollywood elite are. I've got them in my sights." Is asked, "Who are they, specifically?" Says, "They know who they are."

June 15

Quayle holds spelling bee at Trenton, New Jersey, elementary school. Tells 12-year-old William Figueroa, who has just spelled "potato" correctly on blackboard, "You gotta add a little bit at the end there. Spell that again now." Kid spells it correctly again. Quayle says, "Now add one little bit on the end. Think of po-ta-to, how is that spelled? You're right phonetically, but what else...?" Kid capitulates, adds "e," and Quayle says, "There you go!" Beckwith blames misspelling on card Quayle read from. Figueroa says incident "showed the rumors about the vice president are true." What rumors? "That he's an idiot."

June 17

Quayle says he "should have caught the mistake on that spelling bee card. But as Mark Twain once said, 'You should never trust a man who has only one way to spell a word.' " Officials at Mark Twain Museum are unable to find quote. William Figueroa appears on David Letterman show, says that after Quayle left, reporters "were all laughing about what a fool he was."

June 18

Marilyn Quayle expresses "complete and total irritation" at media delight in "potato" gaffe: "He gives five speeches a day for 25 months, never makes a mistake. He makes one mistake and they air, air and air it."

June 19

Quayle, attacking "cultural elite" on *MacNeil/Lehrer News Hour*, again declines to identify them: "They know who they are. (laughs) And I know who they are....The American people know exactly who I'm talking about. The cultural elite know who I'm talking about....We all know that it's there. And it's not going to serve my purpose to go in and to name who's in and who's out....You know a cultural elitist when you see one (laughs uproariously)." Admits he "should have caught the mistake on the spelling bee card," says, "The kid is a smart kid....The kid, he knew *exactly* how to spell it. The press run out to see what the spelling really is. They (chuckles) have to look it up in the dictionary! (chuckles) But the kid knew. The kid's smart."

June 22

President Bush, asked by Barbara Walters who Quayle has in mind when he refers to "cultural elite," says, "I hope he's not talking about me."

June 25

Specially revised opening to *Simpsons* rerun features Bart writing on blackboard "potato not potatoe." Creator Matt Groening says, "Quayle says he wears scorn and ridicule like a badge, so we wanted to help deputize him."

June 27
Bush's daughter remarries. Quayles not invited to wedding.

July 1
House votes to cut all financing for Quayle's Council on Competitiveness.

July 2
Quayle claims Bush broke no-new-taxes pledge because he needed to focus on crisis in Middle East, though, in fact, invasion of Kuwait occurred several weeks *after* tax hike was agreed to.

July 7
Quayle appears on Rush Limbaugh's radio show, says, "Our trick, our trick, Rush is—not trick, our challenge—our challenge is to make sure that the American people feel comfortable with the leadership that George Bush will offer for the next four years." Limbaugh tells him "there is so much love for you out there...so much appreciation for the fact that you have taken this onslaught of abuse...you have more support out there than you know."

July 9
NBC News/*Wall Street Journal* poll shows 50% of Americans view Quayle negatively, 66% are "uncomfortable" with idea of him as president—his worst ratings yet in this poll.

July 13
Democratic Convention opens in New York. Buttons with Quayle's face crossed out over the slogan "JUST SAY NOE" sell out instantly.

July 15
Media reports that note Quayle sent to Sam Snead after golfing with him in 1991 began: "Sam, had a great time this weekend but the golf was lousey."

July 16
Anti-abortion group distributes pro-Quayle literature outside Democratic Convention, spells his name "Quale."

★ ★ ★

William Figueroa, the student who spelled "potato" right, leads convention in Pledge of Allegiance.

July 21

ABC News/*Washington Post* poll shows 63% of Americans view Quayle negatively—his worst rating yet in this poll—and 60% would "approve" of Bush dumping him from GOP ticket.

July 22

Marilyn Quayle blames husband's poor polls on media conspiracy, says, "Polls are done to get a certain result. I've had copies of polls that have been smuggled to me from members of the press where the actual poll data is far different than what comes out in the media. It is selectively produced."

★ ★ ★

Bush says Quayle's place on ticket is "very certain." Media speculation on his dumping intensifies.

★ ★ ★

Quayle tells Larry King he'd support "whatever decision" his daughter made—including abortion—if she were to become pregnant.

July 23

Marilyn Quayle attempts to calm uproar over husband's sudden willingness to make significant exception to anti-abortion views, says daughter would "take the child to term" if she got pregnant. Is asked if she will make that decision for daughter, replies, "We will make it with her."

★ ★ ★

Columnist George Will suggests Bush replace Quayle with Colin Powell.

July 24

Columnist William F. Buckley, Jr. suggests Bush replace Quayle with Jack Kemp.

★ ★ ★

Quayle meets with Bush, is asked afterward if he's staying on ticket. Says, "Yes," calls issue "a closed matter."

July 26
Chicago Tribune urges Bush to dump Quayle: "Hardly any American can be comfortable with the thought that Quayle could become president....That job requires more than ordinary talent; nothing about Quayle rises above the ordinary." Cartoon shows Bush, with Quayle on his back, saying, "No, I'll be carrying him to term." *New York Newsday* urges Bush to dump Quayle: "There is nothing about him that generates respect."

July 30
Former Florida GOP chairman calls Quayle an "albatross," takes out full-page ad in *Washington Post* urging him to resign from ticket.

The authors regret that this book had to go to press the first week of August, thus preventing the inclusion of all the entertainment Quayle will doubtlessly provide on the campaign trail.

November 1992
Revised edition of *Bartlett's Familiar Quotations* includes Quayle's "What a waste it is to lose one's mind."

HAIL FELLOW WELL MET

On his handshake, his wit, his oratorical skills

"The deficiency he exudes goes well beyond intelligence per se. He's just a generally out-of-his-depth guy....He greets you with a rote, dishrag handshake and fuzzy eye contact reminiscent of Katharine Ross in *The Stepford Wives*. Then he sits down and fails to make passable small talk. He occasionally tells a dopey joke, and, when somebody tells a good one, he grasps it roughly two seconds after everyone else; once he even echoed the punch line in less subtle terms, as if anyone but him needed to have it boiled down."

—*Robert Wright*, New Republic

"Watching and listening up close, I saw nothing to suggest that if his brains were made of TNT they would generate enough explosive power to disarrange his hair."

—*Christopher Hitchens*, Harper's

"Ask him to turn off a light, and by the time he gets to the switch, he's forgotten what he went for."

—*Joseph Canzeri, Quayle campaign aide*

"The education of Dan Quayle has worked, sort of. Ask Quayle about any subject he's been briefed on...and he will have a reasonable answer. But ask him to reflect on his own, and the new vice president is still in trouble. He will look earnestly at his questioner, pause reflectively, begin a thoughtful-sounding response, and then say something bordering on the banal."

—*Lynn Rosellini*, U.S. News & World Report

"He treats language like a Lego set, taking a phrase, repeating and building on it, often without regard to meaningful content....He calls to mind the movie *Big*, in which Tom Hanks played a 13-year-old trapped in an adult's body."

—*Maureen Dowd*, New York Times

THE COUNCIL ON COMPETITIVENESS

The dangerous side of dimwit Dan

Contrary to what many Americans believe, Dan Quayle actually has a job. No, it's not being vice president; we all know *that's* not a job. The job Quayle has—the only actual, not titular, task George Bush has given him—is the chairmanship of the President's Council on Competitiveness.

AN ORWELLIAN MISNOMER

What is this council? Is it, like Japan's Ministry of International Trade and Industry (MITI), a way to help domestic industries stay competitive in the world marketplace? Well...no. The Council on Competitiveness—whose name is as boldly misleading as that of the Ministry of Peace in Orwell's *1984*—is not concerned with international competitiveness but with overturning or undermining health, safety and environmental regulations that stand in the way of corporate profits. The competition that the council concerns itself with is not between American and foreign industries but between American industries and American citizens.

Among the council's proudest accomplishments:

• It rejected a ban on the burning of toxic lead batteries;
• It caused the EPA to miss two deadlines for setting airborne toxin guidelines, causing a billion extra pounds of toxins to be released into the air;
• It backed the Labor Department's plan to end a ban on garment workers doing piecework at home;
• It rejected an EPA recycling initiative on the grounds that it competed with a distinguished crony in the private sector: the incinerator industry!;
• At the behest of the biotechnology industry, and despite the support of every other participant, it scuttled U.S. support for an international treaty on biodiversity at the Rio summit;
• It delayed a regulation protecting workers exposed to formaldehyde;

• It fought to withdraw protection from millions of acres of wetlands;

• It eased airport noise restrictions;

• It blocked, stalled or undermined provisions of the Clean Air Act of 1990 which, perversely, Quayle continues to tout as the centerpiece of the administration's environmental effort. For example, a recent Bush-sponsored, council-backed loophole allows a company to increase the amount of pollution it pumps into the atmosphere by up to 245 tons a year without submitting to hearings as required by the Clean Air Act;

• Finally, in January of this year the council mandated a 90-day regulatory moratorium, subsequently extended to 120 days. An analysis of the initial 90-day period by Public Citizen and OMB Watch revealed that at least 43 regulations had been delayed and six weakened or killed, including one requiring a warning label on a type of toy responsible for the death of 186 children over the past decade.

According to every poll, Americans overwhelmingly recognize that Dan Quayle is not the brightest bulb in the hardware store. What the council's sordid record demonstrates is that a dim individual can still be a dangerous individual.

FOXES IN THE HENHOUSE

How does the council work? When watchdog agencies such as the Food and Drug Administration, the Occupational Safety and Health Administration or the Environmental Protection Agency turn down a company's request to eliminate regulations, the Council on Competitiveness can step in and overrule the watchdogs. This sneaky little enterprise has even gained approval authority over Environmental Protection guidelines, as you might have inferred from the above list. This means that if the council —on behalf of one of its industry friends—disapproves of a new EPA rule, it can simply withhold its seal of approval until the rule is revised to an acceptable level of toothlessness.

Never authorized by Congress, and funded from the vice president's office budget, the council refuses to disclose to the public or Congress which groups or industry officials it has met with, which regulations it has meddled with, what evidence it has reviewed. (Other federal regulatory agencies must conduct their business in the open, meet with all sides, attempt to make decisions based on the merits, and generally eschew the type of highhanded behavior associated with Latin American dictatorships.) It refuses Freedom of Information requests, claiming it is "not a government agency" and that it is shielded by "executive privilege."

FOLLOW THE MONEY
Why is the Bush administration so keen on dismantling safeguards that were obviously devised to protect the majority of our citizens from the minority who would gladly harm the rest of us for a profit? The answer can be found in Deep Throat's admonition to "follow the money."

Wherever in the country top administration officials travel, they invariably find time in their hectic schedules to powwow with local businesspeople who happen to be big Republican contributors. It should come as no surprise that Dan Quayle, the one top administration official with little in the way of an official job description, spends an inordinate amount of time jetting around and brown-nosing for dollars.

So: Quayle meets with Republican tycoons, hears them whine about the onerous regulations that are making their lives miserable, promises he'll do something about it, scoops up their checks, and leaves. Back in Washington—and here's the beauty part—*he actually does everything they ask him to do.* Hey, he's in charge of the council that's in charge of the regulatory process—who's going to stop him?

Of course, these powwows occur inside the Beltway as well as on the road; they may be attended by industry lobbyists rather than, or in addition to, corporate principals; and Quayle himself does not personally attend every one—he does, after all, have Easter egg rolls to officiate, golf to play and speeches to mangle.

CONFLICT? WHAT CONFLICT?
The Council on Competitiveness doesn't just help people seeking regulatory relief for their businesses, it is people seeking regulatory relief for their businesses. The council's executive director, Allan B. Hubbard, described as "a wealthy Indiana auto-wax maker," owns chunks of a number of companies that are known polluters. Last November, Senator Al Gore (D-TN) accused Hubbard of a conflict

of interest, asserting that he "has more than $1 million in a company that is polluting the environment, but he is in charge of the regulations governing the pollution." Quayle responded by granting his fellow Hoosier a general waiver of conflict-of-interest rules. Somehow, this didn't make the problem go away. It should be a fun topic for the upcoming Quayle/Gore vice presidential debate.

QUAYLE LEAKS ON HIMSELF

Last year Quayle bragged to Bob Woodward and David Broder of the *Washington Post* that the council leaves "no fingerprints" when it blocks or rewrites regulations, or bullies regulators, for its corporate friends. Obviously this is not entirely true or we wouldn't know as much as we do about the council. One reason so much information is available is that the press is watching: neither George Bush nor Dan Quayle has Ronald Reagan's power to hypnotize reporters. Another reason is that Quayle *wants* to leave fingerprints. The whole point of the Council on Competitiveness is to gain political capital (and fill campaign treasure chests), and how are people going to know you're a tough, pro-business, deregulatory he-man unless you regale them with your deeds?

Upon learning that the job of the council is to unilaterally subvert regulations put in place by duly appointed federal agencies, the first question that comes to most people's minds is: "Can that be legal?" The answer, according to many influential lawmakers, is a resounding "No!" On July 1st of this year the House struck back at Dan Quayle's secret government by voting to eliminate funding for its eight-member staff. The Senate votes the week this book goes to press. With any luck, the council's plug will soon be pulled.

The Council on Competitiveness—in its thuggish boneheadedness, its contempt for due process, and its reflexive kowtowing to the sleaziest, least forward-looking, most self-destructive of business interests—is the perfect organizational embodiment of its chairman, J. Danforth Quayle.

The 1990s will see Japan, an economically united Europe, and the United States scrimmaging to be first with cleaner, greener technologies. The backward approach of Quayle and his accomplices must make our competitors very happy indeed.

HOW TO BEAT HIM IN A DEBATE

F ew Americans above the age of nine would have trouble whipping the vice president in a debate. However, if you don't think you're smarter than Dan Quayle with one lobe tied behind your back—or if you feel you're at a disadvantage due to the 20-year coma you've just emerged from—and you're concerned that circumstances might arise in which Al Gore would ask you to stand in for him on vice presidential debate night, this crib sheet is just for you.

When Quayle says: "Incumbents are out of touch with the folks back home."

You say: "You've been in Washington for 16 years, Dan. Don't you think it's time *you* headed back home?"

When Quayle says: "I'm proud to be associated with George Bush, the Education President."

You say: "Why, then, have you been trying to undermine our public school system—by voting for private-school tuition tax credits—ever since your first term in Congress? How do you square your pro-education rhetoric with the huge cuts in education spending over the Reagan-Bush years? And how do you explain the fact that the president has never once called the chairman of the House Education and Labor Committee to push for a piece of education legislation?"

When Quayle says: "The United States of America is the model of democracy for nations shedding the yoke of Communism."

You say: "Thanks for reminding us of our country's full name again. You claim you're a fan of democracy, and yet your administration has been adamantly opposed to the National Voter Registration Act, the 'motor voter' act, that would open the democratic process to many more people. It seems that democracy is fine with you as long as it doesn't include too many people who are poor, young, Latino or African American."

When Quayle says: "The Hollywood elite is undermining traditional values."

You say: "We notice you reserve your toughest criticism for *Murphy Brown* while saying next to nothing about the thousands of violent deaths the average child sees on television every year. Could it be that you find televised carnage a wholesome substitute for the real kind you missed in Vietnam?"

When Quayle says: "The cultural elite believes that moral truths are relative."

You say: "What Americans believe, fella, is that moral truths are individual, that one's conscience is one's own. Indeed, we consider it un-American when people high up in the government start telling us how to think. Say, isn't that what you conservatives are supposed to believe?"

When Quayle says: "The media elite is out of touch with family values."

You say: "Look, Bozo, it's your administration that's got the vendetta against the American family. You've failed to come up with welfare reforms to help poor families stay together. You've done nothing about the estimated 90,000 children who carry guns to school—nothing but oppose gun control. You oppose family leave legislation, saying it's bad for business. Over the last 21 years, 17 under Republican administrations, the children's poverty rate has doubled—and look at you! You're incapable of doing a thing about it because you're too busy running around kissing corporate butt and squawking about family values!"

When Quayle says: "I didn't pull any strings to get into law school, I got in because of my qualifications."

You say: "POTATO!!"

BOOKS 'N' STUFF

A few moments with America's premier literary tag team

DAN QUAYLE, READER

"You always learn something by reading the classics. Particularly *The Prince*. I go through and look at this from this intellectual point of view....Machiavelli had these three classes of mind.... The first class was the person that was creative enough to be leader and be able to lead a great nation without much help. The second class of mind was one that wasn't creative but could take ideas, put people around him, and be able to lead nations forward. And the third class of people didn't really know much of anything. And they were the worst kind of leaders, because not only were they not creative, but they didn't know what was right or wrong and they just sort of went by whatever they felt like. I've tried to figure out where I am. I know I'm not the first one because I don't think I have that creativeness that Machiavelli talks about. If I go back and reread it I might figure it out exactly where I put myself. I'm somewhere in between two and one."

—*Quayle on Machiavelli's* **The Prince**

"It was a very good book...which shows how people that are really very weird can get into sensitive positions and have a tremendous impact on history."

—*Quayle on Robert Massie's* **Nicholas and Alexandra**

"Well, I think that the concept, you know—you go through how Hitler, you know, grows to power—sees these types of people that are able to feed on the moment—how he has a huge popular support in Germany at the time. It got into the whole, the arms control aspect, and the decline of the defense posture before World War II. He has a very good—and it was something I hadn't thought of, and it's not my area of expertise—and that's how the economic, the international economics, played in all these problems that we had in the 20th century. But there is a rise of these totalitarian leaders. Lenin—a lot of good stuff on Lenin and Stalin."

> —*Quayle on Paul Johnson's* Modern Times
> (*which he described as "probably, that is, you know, the best book
> I've certainly read…a very good historical book about history"*)

MARILYN QUAYLE, WRITER

For your reading pleasure, an excerpt from Embrace the Serpent, *a book by Marilyn T. Quayle and Nancy T. Northcott:*

"She heard the door close behind her, but her eyes were held by the gaunt figure before her, her husband, José. José really was standing before her….They pulled apart slightly, each needing to see the other's face, to reassure himself. José, José, Ines's mind sang. It really was he….Their eyes closed as they pressed their bodies together fiercely. Ines could feel her husband's bones digging into her. How thin he'd become! She knew he must be discovering the same about her….He'd aged terribly, but the light of hope was in his eyes, she saw with gladness.

" 'And you, my sweet one,' Moya said, running his finger lightly over her lips, 'you're lovelier even than my dreams of you….Oh, my darling,' he whispered, one hand caressing her face, his other arm holding her protectively, 'I want to hold you, to feel your nearness. You're so dear to me, so truly precious. But…' His arm tightened. 'As always, we've so little time.'

"Ines pulled back gently from the circle of his arm. 'You're right, of course, but be prepared when the time's finally ours.' The light of mischief sparkled in her gray eyes."

WHAT WE TALK ABOUT WHEN WE TALK ABOUT QUAYLE

Between January and July of 1992 the authors spoke or corresponded with nearly 200 Quayle observers. Here are the highlights of those exchanges.

Why Bush Chose Him

"I think the reason Bush chose him is that the Busher is in love with youth. That's why he's always saying things like 'zippity doo-dah' and so on. There's something infantilist about Bush, and this was what responded so murkily in him to Quayle's hideous, beaming, stupid, youthful face."

—*Martin Amis, author,*
Money, London Fields, Time's Arrow

His Soulfulness

"Dan Quayle is so white he probably says 'The powers that are.'"
—*Charlie Haas, writer*

His Earthiness

"I like him a lot. He's very straight ahead, very direct, almost what I call a street person....I've greeted President Reagan, President Bush, and I've greeted him. And he was the most earthy, with a lot of humor."

—*Sonny Bono, former mayor, Palm Springs, California*

How He Reminds Us of Certain Boys We Knew in School

"He seems like the kind of guy who would throw a snowball at you but if you threw one back at him he'd probably burst out crying and run home to tell his father. And there'd be repercussions."
—*Rosie Schuster, screen and TV writer*

He Reminds Us of Certain Copycats We Knew in School

"He has the face of a guy who wants to copy from your paper. I'll bet you a hundred bucks he copied in class."

—Lynn Snowden, journalist

How Like a Burger King Manager He Is

"It's a little cheesy to criticize Dan Quayle for being a moron—the whole point of the Reagan era was to put stupid rich people in power. They're all over the place now; there are 500,000 Dan Quayles. Everybody who works for a Burger King works for a Dan Quayle."

—Ian Frazier, author, The Great Plains

How There's Finally a Number to Call to Report People Who Say Bad Things About Him

"The purpose of Friends of Dan Quayle is to promote the fair and balanced presentation of his tasks and accomplishments. You can get in touch with us when you see things you don't like that the press is doing to him: just call our answering machine, tell us about it, and we'll check it out. The number is 202-508-1448."

—John Piper, president, Friends of Dan Quayle

How His Avoidance of Combat Service Embarrasses Those Who Opposed the Vietnam War on Moral and/or Ethical and/or Political Grounds

"He gives draft dodgers a bad name."

—Joe Bodolai, Canadian TV producer
and former American draft dodger

His Unusual Manner of Speech

"My theory is that he wears a tiny radio receiver and earphone concealed by his Robert Redford wig. Close by, in an unmarked van full of transmitting equipment, are a bunch of speechwriters feeding him information, like Steve Martin in *Roxanne*. Everything goes OK until, say, a car passes with a cellular phone, which jams the frequency and he hears—and repeats—random lines. That's when you get stuff like 'What a waste it is to lose one's mind.'"

—Ernie Fosselius, filmmaker and satirist

His Spelling Disability

"There is a tailor shop in Indianapolis, Leon Tailoring, with an autographed photo of Quayle on the wall which he signed 'To Leon, my favorite Taylor,' spelled T-a-y-l-o-r. Now, I don't know what Leon's last name is, but it's definitely not Taylor."

—*Professor Paul J. Galanti,*
Indiana University School of Law/Indianapolis

His Intelligence vis-a-vis That of Another Recent American Statesman

"Dan Quayle is more stupid than Ronald Reagan put together!"

—*Matt Groening, creator of* The Simpsons

How We Figure It's Going to Be Quayle-D'Amato in '96

"There's this succession of infinitely diminishing Republicans, starting with Reagan. Everybody said we can't impeach Reagan 'cause we'd just get Bush, and everybody says we hope nothing happens to Bush 'cause we'll get Quayle, and then when Quayle gets in...it's fascinating to imagine somebody Quayle can pick for his running mate who would cause us to say we can't impeach Quayle, we'd only get you-know-who."

—*Roy Blount, Jr., author,* First Hubby

What a Good Place He's In

"I've worked with Dan Quayle since I came here. I've watched him grow, I've watched him mature. I see that fleck of white at his temples, I see a guy who looks much more comfortable with himself.... He becomes more impressive every time I see him, and I have no problem picturing him as president....He's taken some hard shots, taken them with great grace. There isn't anything more you can dish out to him, and that's a good place for a human being to be, when you've had every truckload of trash dumped over your head and damn near come up to your neck, and you just pry your way out and keep right on living. It can't get any worse for him."

—*Senator Alan K. Simpson (R-WY)*

The Allegation That He's Dyeing His Temples Gray to Look More Distinguished

"It's not true. His temples have been graying for about four years. Look, these rumors tend to get into the folklore. In 1989 the *Washington Post* ran an editorial criticizing eight different magazines that had published, as fact or reported fact, that story about Quayle on a Latin American trip saying he regretted not speaking Latin. The *Post* pointed out that this began as a joke in a [former Republican Congresswoman] Claudine Schneider dinner speech, but these publications picked it up as fact. Believe it or not, that Latin story is still around. He was in London recently and was asked about it in all seriousness by a BBC interviewer who thought he had actually said it.

"I'm very interested in not having more things like that get started, so if I can help you check the accuracy of any of this stuff I'd be happy to."

—*David Beckwith, Quayle's press secretary*

The Most Interesting Thing We Know About Him

"I wrote a humor column for *The Nation*, a fictionalized diary of a high-level bureaucrat in the Bush White House. In one of my articles I made up a Quayle quote. He was giving a speech to the VFW, and I had him say: 'The Civil War was the best war we've ever had because when you're fighting with yourself you're always going to win.' About two weeks later I got a call from the *Quayle Quarterly*. They'd had numerous calls from people who thought it was a real quote and wanted to have it verified. Which is pretty amazing, really. But you know, if you put that quote in the middle of a bunch of real Quayle quotes you wouldn't even blink. It's the most interesting thing I know about Quayle: you can make up any quote, the more ridiculous the better, and it'll sound real."

—*Douglas G. McGrath, columnist/playwright/screenwriter*

How Having Nothing to Say Affects the Way He Says It

"He's tongue-tied in a way that only someone with nothing to say can be."

—*Mark O'Donnell, humorist/playwright/author*

How Thinking About Him Puts Us in Mind of a Lot of Things That Make Our Skin Crawl

"J. Danforth Quayle, that dangling initial tells the story: the pompous self-importance of your small town banker who forecloses the farm, your Gulf War general with the $5 million advance whose selective chronicle of slaughter is being written by someone else; J. Danforth Quayle, the acolyte of the reigning prince of hypocrites (two patrician middle initials this time): J. Danforth Quayle, who has in fact got principles of his own, derived from an abiding confusion of an elitism based on merit, with a Midwestern country club version embracing the empty privileges of unearned money; and who is not the public joke so frequently portrayed but rather, in being smart rather than intelligent, using the vested interests that are using him, could if allowed by a skipped heartbeat or a dazed electorate, emerge as quite a dangerous fellow."

—*William Gaddis, author,*
The Recognitions, JR, Carpenter's Gothic

Why Bush Chose Him: Another Possibility

"All of his knowledge seems to be received knowledge; he seems to have no defined self. There's a cultural emptiness there. There's no there there. But he's not the problem. It's politics by imagery that's the problem—he was selected strictly for his image, which is a kind of stereotype of whites, certainly from the point of view of minorities. Blond and shallow and golf-playing and essentially indifferent to other people."

—*Shelby Steele, author,* The Content of Our Character

The Effing Media

"I believe Dan Quayle has a good temperament, a real political philosophy, consistency—yet not a single journalist in three years attempted to do a serious piece on him. Period. And the fucking media know it. The first semi-balanced piece was Woodward and Broder. Everything before that was cartoonlike, caricature, jokes, Johnny Carson…more hits, more innuendoes. The media in this country are totally fucking out of control, they really are."

—*Roger Ailes, 1988 Bush-Quayle campaign consultant*

How, After Reading the Interminable Woodward/Broder Series in the *Washington Post,* We Think Much More Highly of Him...Not!

"I think the Right breathed a sigh of relief that there were no examples of him talking to his rubber duckie. But anyone else who looked at the piece objectively would say, all right, the guy's not a moron, but what qualifies him for the presidency?"

—*Richard Cohen,* Washington Post *columnist*

Why He's Worth 40,000 Words (in 200 Words or Less)

"Quayle could be president tomorrow, and we ought to know who he is. If the series is confusing to people, if it doesn't reduce him to one line, if it's not the kind of bombshell-oriented writing that sometimes I've been associated with—that's what it is. That's who he is. At least now there's a record, a definitive version. Did we answer all the questions? No. Did we answer lots of them? I believe we did. Is it too soft? No, I don't think so. At one point, for instance, we show how he spent six months working secretly to get picked as Bush's running mate, yet when he was picked—without even being interviewed for the job—he had no idea what to say. None! I think that's highly critical, but it's presented just the way life is lived: in context.

"I feel totally comfortable with the series. It's exactly what reporters should do. This idea that we shouldn't have knowledge about Dan Quayle—I just don't get it."

—*Bob Woodward,* Washington Post *assistant managing editor and co-author,* The Man Who Would Be President: Dan Quayle

How Gauging His Fitness to Be President Is Different from Investigating a Third-Rate Break-In

"The problem with the Woodward/Broder piece is that by using the usual journalistic techniques—the ones you'd use to prove or disprove someone's guilt in the Watergate break-in—you cannot prove or disprove whether someone's an ass. The polls that consistently show Americans don't believe Dan Quayle is qualified to be president reflect a conviction not based on anything provable or actionable but on the judgment that he is a vacuous, insubstantial and rather fatuous person. Where do Woodward and Broder get the idea that we must take buffoons as seriously as we take everybody else?"

—*Robert Reno,* Newsday *columnist*

How Much We Gals Go for Him

"Ordinarily you don't see people focusing on a male politician's looks. It seems to weaken them if they're seen as a pretty boy. But that's what everyone was saying about Quayle in '88: Bush was tossing the girls a bone, giving them a cute guy to hang on their walls like a Robert Redford eight-by-ten glossy.

"For the most Pollyannaish, or delusionary, this may be seen as a step toward equality. Of course, that theory falls apart when you look at Quayle's actual record, rather than his baby blue eyes. He's never taken a single stance that's especially friendly to women, which is why it was no surprise that the Bush-Quayle ticket actually did worst with unmarried, 'available' women—an amusing rebuttal to Bush's 'cutie' campaign strategy."

—*Susan Faludi, author,*
Backlash: The Undeclared War Against American Women

How Much We Gals Go for Him, Part II

"He has the kind of personality that women just steer clear of. Men like that, with chips on their shoulders, put out this thing that's like screaming radar—you can spot them from 20 feet away, just by their body language, and you hope never to have to talk to them.... He feels incompetent and telegraphs it constantly. I saw him on CNN today. He looked like he was trying to imitate Kennedy, but he kept falling out of it—it was like watching an actor lose his character. He'd get agitated about something he didn't have a rehearsed response for, forget his composure, and become Dan Quayle again, all wide-eyed and goofy. Next thing you know, he's making some joke that reveals his stupidity even to himself and hurls him back into inferiority hell. Poor thing."

—*Lisa Ferguson, actress/singer/writer*

His Alleged Resemblance to Redford

"He's like Redford's retarded brother that they kept up in the attic, and he got out somehow."

—Patty Marx, writer

How He'd Be a Director's Nightmare

"An intelligent actor can play a stupid person with some degree of success, but a stupid actor can never play an intelligent character. This is why Quayle's performance never works: he just doesn't look real. If I were directing him, I'd have him go for the Gary Cooper I'm-a-naive-bumbler-and-none-too-bright-but-I-know-what's-right-'cause-I'm-a-man-of-the-people persona. The problem is, Quayle is not a man of the people. He's a rich kid. Rich and stupid is real tough. I'd probably recast."

—Eric Loeb, playwright/director

How He Might Be Smarter Than We're Capable of Imagining

"In school, the smartest kids always seemed a little awkward and weird. By these standards, he could be the most brilliant human who ever lived. Maybe there's so much information up there that he's just overloaded."

—Arleen Sorkin, writer/producer/actress

How We Can't Imagine Anyone Stupider

"There's a scene in my novel where the presidential candidate, Governor Ross, is talking to his advisers about Brent Bibby, his extremely stupid running mate. An adviser says that Bibby—who they've sent on a tour of small-town grade schools—has made a big mistake in a spelling bee. Ross asks if it was a hard word, like *phlegm*. The adviser says, 'No, it was *house*. He put a W in it.' Ross says, 'Well, you can sort of see that, can't you: H-O-W-S-E?' 'Unfortunately sir,' the adviser says, 'he placed the W at the beginning.'

"Back in January, when I was writing the book, this was the stupidest thing I could think of. I got a little panicky at Quayle's 'potatoe' incident—everyone will think I stole my scene from the real event. When in fact art preceded life."

> —*Jamie Malanowski, national editor of* Spy *magazine and author,* Mr. Stupid Goes to Washington

How Even Though He Wasn't Too Good in School He's Grown Up to Be a World-Class Brown-Noser

"He spent a fair amount of time when he was a senator asking Bush's opinion on defense and CIA and so forth. In other words, he's somebody who would have impressed Bush as being interested in Bush's ideas. Now, there's not a huge list of people who were interested in his ideas back when he was not expressing them, because he was subordinated to Reagan. Bush just didn't say very much back then, publicly.

"Dan Quayle is probably not a bad political strategist in terms of advancing Dan Quayle. The record would suggest, if you judge him on that, that he's entitled to a fair amount of respect."

> —*Kevin Phillips, GOP analyst and publisher,* The American Political Report

His Brown-Nosing, Part II

"Every time he talks about George Bush he makes him sound like Mr. Rogers, or like a favorite teacher—the only one who ever gave him a good grade."

> —*George Malko, screenwriter/novelist*

His Brown-Nosing, Part III

"He's using his office as a platform for winning brownie points from the big business groups that are funding the Bush-Quayle campaign and, heaven forbid, a future Quayle presidential campaign. As chairman of the Council on Competitiveness, he's nothing more than the in-house lobbyist for the Fortune 500 against the reasonable health and safety rights of the American people."

> —*Ralph Nader, founder, Public Citizen*

How He's No Gerald Ford...

"On the occasion of the succession of a vice president—whether

through death or assassination or, in a single case, resignation—
the country goes into a period of trauma. It can be very dangerous if
the vice president is not perceived as someone capable of having a
calming effect and getting the country through that period.

"Both Lyndon Johnson and, to a lesser degree, Jerry Ford, when
they ascended to the presidency, were perceived as being capable of
handling the situation. Quayle's problem is that he's not remotely
so perceived. I think shock waves would go through the country if
we woke up tomorrow morning and found that Dan Quayle was
president."

—*Jules Witcover, author,*
Crapshoot: Rolling the Dice on the Vice Presidency

...But He Just Might Be Another Richard Nixon

"Is he on track to be president? Yes, I think so, and people ought to
deal with it. What Nixon figured out is that it makes no difference
how bad your record is, or how many pages of Dubious Achieve-
ments you come up with: if you raise enough money you'll win.
And Quayle will raise the money because he's been the defender of
the fat cats, and they'll fund him. He's going to walk out there and
say, 'I'm the new Dan Quayle.' Just like the new Nixon."

—*Representative Pat Schroeder (D-CO)*

How We Loathe the Sound of His Voice

"A Dan Quayle speech debases anybody in the world who has ever
honestly used passion in oratory. He's convinced that the louder
and more forcefully he says something, the more belief he can
churn up in listeners, but since he has no understanding of the
meaning of what he's saying, anybody who is in touch with his or
her feelings, whether it's an adult or a small child, instantly recog-
nizes that voice as fundamentally phony—the voice of a spoiled,
petulant sixth-grader telling a lie, a country-club kid desperately
trying to simulate the sound of political belief. He's like a horrible
trumpet player driving all the air through his lungs and mouth that
he can, but instead of getting anything approaching music, these
metallic nasal *blaaats* come out, this tinny flatulence. His voice—
with all of its condescending smugness and synthetic passion, totally devoid of any intelligence or soul, like a hot-wired HAL from

2001—turns all of American politics into a humorless audio parody of itself, making you madder and madder the more you listen to it, until you want to come at him with a two-by-four and scream, 'Stop it! Stop it! Stop it now!' "

—*Peter W. Kaplan, writer/editor*

How Fascinating It Would Be to Know What He's Really Thinking

"Just before the inauguration I visited the Naval Observatory, where the vice presidents live, to do a *Sports Illustrated* story about George Bush and horseshoes. After we'd finished playing horseshoes the president-elect took me inside for a tour. In the front hall, where various cabinet members were getting ready for a meeting, Sununu looked at me and said, 'Aha, so you're going to be vice president for a couple of days.' Which pleased me enormously, since he knew about the participatory journalism stints I do in life. And there was Dan Quayle, with that startled-deer look that everybody talks about, which I'd never seen before. He was staring at me. I don't think he had any idea who I was; it crossed my mind that he actually thought I *was* going to take over his job for a couple of days. Or even, with the election over, that the president was going to kick him off the ticket and replace him with me. Back to the Senate with you! Not so, of course, but certainly he seemed quite stunned."

—*George Plimpton, author*

How Inappropriately Smug He Is, Given His Inarticulateness

"I don't understand how someone as inarticulate as he is can be so smug."

—*Maren Jensen, actress*

How Hard It Is to Bond with Him

"Dan Quayle and I played in the fall of '89. It was for a series we have called '18 Holes With...,' the theory being that you can learn a lot about someone by playing 18 holes of golf with him. I didn't expect to become his best friend, but he was awfully aloof—I'd hoped for a little more golfer bonding, especially since he and I had very similar games. Plus, we were partners against two other guys.

"It was raining and I arrived without any rain gear. In the course of the 18 holes, my partner was the only one among the golfers and caddies who never offered to share his umbrella with me. In his defense, he was nice to even come out and play, given the conditions —it says something about his being as much of a golf nut as I am. But you know, by the 18th hole I wanted to beat him more than I wanted the two of us to beat our opponents."

—*George Peper, editor-in-chief,* Golf *magazine*

How, By Golly, We Just Can't Say Enough About What a Super Guy He Is!

"You have to take into consideration how old he was when he was selected....Was he as mature at 42 as he is now? No. Nobody is. He's naturally going to grow. There's been tremendous growth.... But he also was a substantial individual when he was picked...he had plenty of skill...but he also worked hard....He's a very bright guy who works hard and plays hard, too....

"He is very underrated by the press...I don't think most of the criticisms are justified....I believe part of it is because most people did not expect him to be selected as vice president....There are people who are downright jealous of him. There are people who will knock anybody who has a position above theirs....You got a media that's out to get him, some people are jealous of him, you got some who just plain don't have a good thing to say about anybody, and you add to that people who have axes to grind and you're going to get some criticism....

"Can I see him as president? I sure can, let me tell you. One of the cabinet officials who traveled with him during the '88 presidential campaign said that wherever he went huge crowds came, people just fell in love with the guy, and they went berserk when he was around because they like him. They like his appearance, they like the way he talks, they like the conservatism that he manifests....

"I think one reason that President Bush did as well as he did in New Hampshire [in the 1992 Republican primary, where he garnered a pitiful 53% of the vote] was because of Quayle's campaigning. He wasn't afraid to get in there and shake hands....I think he has a very charming approach....He's an asset....Wherever he goes, especially young people—a large group the president had a little difficulty with when he was running for president—and especially women, and I think mature males, they say they go for Dan Quayle very well...."

—*Senator Orrin G. Hatch (R-UT)*

How He Unites Democrats and Republicans

"Was he an esteemed member of the United States Senate who only later got into trouble? I can only tell you that the immediate reaction I heard from insiders, in August of 1988, to the choice of Dan Quayle was bewilderment and, depending on which side of the aisle they were on, joy or chagrin. I talked to dozens of people in Washington who knew him, and they all said the equivalent of 'this guy is a joke.' During the debate negotiations everybody would make Quayle jokes—Democrats and Republicans. It was probably the only subject on which both sides agreed."

—*Susan Estrich, manager of the Dukakis-Bentsen campaign*

How, Despite Everything, We Keep Finding Reasons to Like Him

"I have a very good impression of Dan Quayle. I've heard him speak, I've met him many times, I think he's solid and I like him. Of course, I like men who stick with their first wife."

—*Phyllis Schlafly, anti-abortion crusader and president of Eagle Forum*

Our Fantasy About Him

"Dan Quayle is giving a speech about the National Endowment of the Arts, and he has that spacy, wide-eyed Ken doll look, like he was just whacked in the back of the head with a two-by-four real hard, and he's going on about the shame of funding piss art, and he keeps mentioning piss art, over and over again.

"And suddenly, Squeaky Fromme, out on parole, stabs him 231 times before finally being subdued by security. Frankly, it's almost as if security really didn't give a fuck. They dawdle, they discuss how much force to use, play a couple of hands of poker, and then finally take her down.

"They lay Dan out on the pavement and, wouldn't you know it, a big steamroller comes along and just turns him into a rug mat—such a good rug mat that it seems a shame to bury him, particularly in these times of recession when we have to make every little bit count.

"So they slice him up in strips of beef jerky and send him off as part of the Russian relief program. So even now, there is some sheepherder in the Urals chewing on a strip of Dan Quayle—yum, yum—and thinking inexplicably something about piss art, how wrong it is, how we shouldn't fund it."

—*Michael O'Donoghue, writer*

How We'd Use Him and Bush as Democratic Poster Boys

"Picture a split-screen—two images, no words. On the left you have Bush, passed out with his mouth hanging open; on the right, a rosy-cheeked, perky, smiling Quayle."

—*Neil Levy, screenwriter*

Why Bush Chose Him: Yet Another Possibility

"It may be this medication Bush was on. He was at the convention, he was in an excitable state, they put him on these mood-altering drugs, Roger Ailes stepped up and said, 'You know, this Dan Quayle is a good-looking young guy. Women'll vote for him.' And Bush said, 'Hey, right, Quayle.' "

—*Julian Bond, Distinguished Adjunct Professor in Residence at American University, Washington D.C.*

His Possible Place in History

"Dan Quayle is the penumbra that hangs over the end of the 20th Century. Is there anything in Revelations about a blond mental defective bringing about the end of the world?"

—*Dr. Kerry K. Willis, editor of scientific books and journals*

WHAT QUAYLE TALKS ABOUT WHEN HE TALKS ABOUT QUAYLE

His Decision-Making Ability

"I don't worry about things. My problem is that sometimes I act too quickly and I'll make a mistake. But if I do, my attitude is, 'I'll fix that up when I get to it....' Some people spend a lot of time thinking, 'Should I do this or that?' I don't. I just decide what I want to do and do it. I don't go over and over decisions. My wife does, but I don't. It's a matter of self-confidence."

How He Came to Work in the Consumer Protection Division of the Indiana Attorney General's Office

"It was just a job. It wasn't any special interest in consumer affairs. I needed a paycheck and the attorney general said that I would be best to go down there, because he knew I was anti-consumer."

His Musical Preferences

"Some reporter asked me who I liked better, Jim Morrison or Jimi Hendrix. I hadn't heard of Jim Morrison, so I took Jimi Hendrix."

His Developmental Tardiness

"I'm a classic late bloomer. Some develop a sense of seriousness earlier in life than others. I was clearly late in that category."

The Effect on Him of Huge Heaps of Public Scorn

"They say I've lost a certain easiness, a degree of self-confidence. I'm not sure. Obviously, if you've gone through what I've gone through, you've got to ask some basic questions that force you to be extremely introspective."

DECODING DANNY: A GLOSSARY OF QUAYLISMS

Cultural Elite: Those who are not big Republican contributors or have not been "born again" or are not members of the John Birch Society or would not invite Phyllis Schlafly to dinner or have IQs over 85.

Family: 1. "A wife and three children, a larger family with grandparents and aunts and uncles...," that is, in Dan Quayle's personal language, "family" means Dan Quayle's family. 2. Something "we have in our platform...to talk about."

Family Values: Dan Quayle's family values.

God: The head of the conservative wing of the Republican party.

Hollywood Elite: Those who subvert traditional values by refusing to portray all Americans as happy white nuclear families living in the suburbs.

Media Elite: Those who work for media outlets not owned by members of Quayle's family or Reverend Sun Myung Moon.

Potato: Trick spelling-bee question.

Special Interests: The nefarious masterminds behind the Democratic party who are fighting for such evils as the right to unionize, a cleaner environment, better public schooling, and an end to Dan Quayle's political career.

Temperamental Tycoon: 1. A presidential candidate who is a liar, a crypto-fascist, and a baby killer. 2. A distinguished former presidential candidate whose values are almost precisely those of the Bush-Quayle ticket.

Traditional Values: A code of behavior largely inferred from *Ozzie and Harriet*, *Leave It to Beaver* and other 1950s sitcoms.

THE CULTURAL ELITE SPEAKS

On his finger wagging, his Agnewism, his Snoopyhood

"For Dan Quayle, of all people, to be giving instruction on how poor people must buckle down and get their values together and pull themselves up by the bootstraps…is, at the very least, ironic and morally klunkish.…Quayle, whose own ascent into the political stratosphere has not exactly been an example of hard work rewarded, should have a little humility about hitting the bootstrap circuit so hard."

—Washington Post *editorial*

"He's the goof-off made good, and when he starts wagging his finger at us, we don't like it."

—*Ann Lewis, Democratic consultant*

"Quayle was born not with a mere silver spoon but with a silver ladle in his mouth.…There is something distinctly unbecoming about Quayle's efforts to present himself as a man of the people."

—*Robert Hughes,* Time

"The most troubling symptom of our national decay is this insane conspiracy to pretend that Dan Quayle is a serious man who makes an occasional ass of himself and that these are exceptions to his behavior and character."

—Robert Reno, Newsday

"Quayle in part plays the Spiro Agnew role to Bush's Richard Nixon. But when Agnew went after the 'nattering nabobs' and student protesters, he did so with a thuggish menace that Quayle lacks. Quayle smacks more of Midwestern Americana, of *The Music Man*'s Professor Harold Hill, and Quayle's lines about unmarried mothers sounded like an echo: 'We got trouble, right here in River City!'—brazen hussies strutting around town in a family way: Make your blood boil? Well, I should say!...Quayle makes much of the theme of the absent father; America under the Bush administration looks like a house with an absent father. A man has no right to abandon the family for years and then show up one day and go upstairs and start spanking the kids."

—*Lance Morrow,* Time

"I like getting lectures on values and hard work from Dan Quayle, who recently charged the taxpayers $27,000 for a golfing weekend."
—*Molly Ivins,* Fort Worth Star-Telegram

"I've always thought of the elite as the sort of people who play golf at snooty country clubs and have so much influence that they can get even their dumbest kid into college."

—*Calvin Trillin,* The Nation

"It isn't moral values that people laugh at, of course—it's Mr. Quayle himself, and it isn't the elite who do the laughing. For four years, Dan Quayle jokes have served to unite Americans of all walks of life and all religious faiths. It's only in Washington he is considered a heavyweight. Elsewhere, he is a comic character, like Snoopy, known by his hair, his face and the look in his eyes—and morality is not what we think of first, second or third, when his name is mentioned. We think, *not too bright.*"

—*Garrison Keillor,* New York Times

"Just because everyone says he's a moron doesn't mean he isn't."
—*Joe Queenan,* GQ

NOTE: *"People in the newspaper business hate the government," Dan Quayle told author Richard Fenno. "It is deeply ingrained in them that the government should keep hands off, that government cannot do any good, that it only brings trouble. That distrust is deeply ingrained in me." It is one of the delightful paradoxes of our enigmatic and complex vice president that he traces his rabid right-wing views to a lifelong membership in the "media elite."*

WHAT'S YOUR QUAYLE QUOTIENT?

Measure your own values against those of America's preeminent moral gadfly, Vice President Dan Quayle!

INSTRUCTIONS

Below you will find ten statements. Read each one carefully, then check the appropriate box to indicate whether you "strongly agree," "agree," "neither agree nor disagree," "disagree," or "strongly disagree" with the statement. Ready? Begin.

1. *I define "family" as a married couple, 3 children, grandparents, and assorted aunts and uncles.*

❏ strongly agree
❏ agree
❏ neither agree nor disagree
❏ disagree
❏ strongly disagree

2. *A woman should not have an abortion even if the pregnancy was the result of rape, and she already has several children, and her welfare has been cut off because she has a part-time job. Having the baby will make her a better person.*

❏ strongly agree
❏ agree
❏ neither agree nor disagree
❏ disagree
❏ strongly disagree

3. *I'm in favor of a clean environment and all, but not if it prevents American industries from making a profit.*

☐ strongly agree
☐ agree
☐ neither agree nor disagree
☐ disagree
☐ strongly disagree

4. *It's very important to tell our kids to study hard, learn to spell, try to read books and so on and so forth, but it's even more important to teach them traditional values, bring them up in a good neighborhood, shield them from bad influences, introduce them to the right people, make sure they have a trust fund, and ask God to send them very good luck.*

☐ strongly agree
☐ agree
☐ neither agree nor disagree
☐ disagree
☐ strongly disagree

5. *There could very well be a special part of hell that is reserved for unmarried women who decide to have children.*

☐ strongly agree
☐ agree
☐ neither agree nor disagree
☐ disagree
☐ strongly disagree

6. *I just don't understand what this problem is that some people have about praying in school. The United States of America was founded by people who prayed in school. If you don't want to pray in school you can just transfer to another school. Or at least stand outside the classroom for a few minutes and don't make everybody else suffer.*

☐ strongly agree
☐ agree
☐ neither agree nor disagree
☐ disagree
☐ strongly disagree

7. *There's one form of birth control even a poor unmarried woman living in our inner cities can afford, and it's not something that's handed out by failed liberal welfare programs, or something that causes you to be promiscuous. I'm talking about a simple, one-syllable word, and that word is "no, thank you."*

- ☐ strongly agree
- ☐ agree
- ☐ neither agree nor disagree
- ☐ disagree
- ☐ strongly disagree

8. *We don't have to point our fingers at them or say their names aloud—the media elite and the cultural elite and the Hollywood elite know exactly who they are. It's a lot like what someone, I don't know who, said about pornography: you know one when you see one.*

- ☐ strongly agree
- ☐ agree
- ☐ neither agree nor disagree
- ☐ disagree
- ☐ strongly disagree

9. *Sex education is not something that should be taught in school. It's something to teach at home. In the warmth and comfort of the family, sitting in the den, around the fireplace, all three children and the mother and father and the wise old grandmother and maybe some aunts and uncles just sitting around discussing the things that matter. We shouldn't be sending the innocence of childhood to school and rubbing its face in condoms and whatnot.*

- ☐ strongly agree
- ☐ agree
- ☐ neither agree nor disagree
- ☐ disagree
- ☐ strongly disagree

10. *The cultural elite is going around saying "family values" is a code for something. Well, we know that "family values" is not a code for anything. "Family values" means exactly what it says it means. Traditional values. Important values that are...important. Values that we have here in the United States of America. And anyone who thinks otherwise, well, you can just vote for someone other than President George Bush, which I certainly don't advise you to do because he understands exactly about the family values that made this nation great.*

❑ strongly agree
❑ agree
❑ neither agree nor disagree
❑ disagree
❑ strongly disagree

TO DISCOVER YOUR QUAYLE QUOTIENT

Score 10 (ten) points for each "strongly agree," 5 (five) points for each "agree," 3 (three) points for each "neither agree nor disagree," 2 (two) points for each "disagree," and 0 (zero) points for each "strongly disagree." Add your points together, using a calculator if necessary.

INTERPRETING YOUR QUAYLE QUOTIENT

100   Perfect score. Quayle caliber!

80-99 Very good. You sure know your values! '

60-79 Passing. Try giving more thought to your values.

40-59 Failing. Where are your values?

20-39 Failing badly. Are you an unwed mother?

2-19   Failing miserably. You're ruining this great nation of ours!

0   YOU LIBERAL ELITIST!

NOTE: *If you scorn us for reducing family values to a silly formula, we will wear your scorn as a badge of honor.*

INDEX

THE AUTHORS

Veteran political humorist **Paul Slansky** is the author of *The Clothes Have No Emperor*, the definitive chronicle of the Reagan years. He has written for dozens of magazines, among them the *New Republic*, *Spy* and *Esquire*, where he was a key contributor to the annual Dubious Achievement awards during the '80s. He is currently writing movies in Los Angeles.

Humor writer and journalist Steve Radlauer contributed to the *Off the Wall Street Journal* and *Irrational Inquirer* parodies, has written film segments for Children's Television Workshop programs, is a contributor to *Spy* magazine, and has authored or co-authored five books including the satirical greeting card collection *Special Moments*.